Lowell Mason

Lowell Mason, 1792-1872 (Artist unknown)

Lowell Mason

A Bio-Bibliography

Carol A. Pemberton

Bio-Bibliographies in Music, Number 11
Donald L. Hixon, Series Adviser

Greenwood Press
New York • Westport, Connecticut • London

Library of Congress Cataloging-in-Publication Data

Pemberton, Carol A. (Carol Ann), 1939-
  Lowell Mason : a bio-bibliography / Carol A. Pemberton.
    p.   cm.—(Bio-bibliographies in music, ISSN 0742-6968 ; no.
11)
  Includes index.
  ISBN 0-313-25881-3 (lib. bdg. : alk. paper)
  1. Mason, Lowell, 1792-1872—Bibliography.   2. Music—United
States—Bio-bibliography.   3. Mason, Lowell, 1792-1872.
4. Composers—United States—Biography.   I. Title.   II. Series.
ML134.M46P4   1988
016.783'092'4—dc19   87-37569

British Library Cataloguing in Publication Data is available.

Library of Congress Catalog Card Number: 87-37569
ISBN: 0-313-25881-3
ISSN: 0742-6968

First published in 1988

Greenwood Press, Inc.
88 Post Road West, Westport, Connecticut 06881

Printed in the United States of America

The paper used in this book complies with the
Permanent Paper Standard issued by the National
Information Standards Organization (Z39.48-1984).

10 9 8 7 6 5 4 3 2 1

Copyright Acknowledgments

The author and publisher gratefully acknowledge the following for permission to
quote copyrighted material:
  Excerpt from *Lowell Mason: His Life and Work*, pp. 223-25, copyright ©
1985, 1971 by Carol A. Pemberton, is reprinted courtesy of UMI Research Press,
Ann Arbor, Michigan.
  George Brandon for his words in a letter to the author, March 6, 1987.
  Arthur L. Rich for his words in a letter to the author, August 20, 1986.
  Excerpt from *"Susanna," "Jeanie," and "The Old Folks at Home": The
Songs of Stephen C. Foster from His Time to Ours*, p. 10, copyright © 1975 by
William W. Austin (Macmillan: New York, 1975) courtesy of the author.

To my mother and dad,

in loving memory

Contents

Preface

Lowell Mason was an American musician who lived from 1792-1872. He is best known as a pioneer music educator and as a composer/arranger of hymn tunes. Since his death, Mason's impact on American music culture has been recognized in many ways by many writers. His admirers and his detractors — and those who strive to remain neutral — agree that Mason's impact on American music culture was enormous, but they disagree over whether that impact was for better or for worse or some of each.

During his lifetime, Lowell Mason was widely known, and with good reason. He had direct contact with thousands of music teachers and students, professional and amateur musicians, and leaders in education, publishing, religion, and politics. He also had indirect contact with hundreds of thousands through his tireless public speaking and his prolific publishing.

After his death, Mason's life and work began to assume some of the qualities of a legend, with all the excesses of praise and narrowness of perspective that accompany legends. There has been a rather understandable tendency to view Mason narrowly as a music educator or as a church musician, rather than to see his career as a mosaic held together by the strong threads of his own objectives.

Full-scale examination of Mason's life and work was long delayed for a number of reasons, some of them suggested in the biographical essay below. In recent years, more research has been published so that Mason's work can be better understood. I hope that this book will inspire, then facilitate further study of Mason and his times; I also hope that the findings will be published, thereby casting more light into our shadowy understanding of nineteenth-century America and American music.

It is particularly fitting that *Lowell Mason: A Bio-Bibliography* should appear in 1988 while American music educators commemorate the sesquicentennial of music in American public schools. Lowell Mason, more than any other one person, is responsible for winning a place for music in the Boston Public School curriculum. Once music had won a place there, a pattern was set: as Boston went, so went other schools systems across the nation in succeeding years.

On August 28, 1838, the Boston School Committee authorized the hiring of a vocal music teacher for the public schools. With the landmark resolution of that day, American public education won a great victory; that resolution was a turning point not only for music in the schools, but also for the concept that the fine arts belong in public education.

Important as that resolution was for music education and for American public education generally, for Lowell Mason, the achievement was but one of many. Various aspects of Mason's career are discussed in various sources, such as those in the bibliography below, but comprehensive views of his career are available in only a few sources, among them *Lowell Mason: His Life and Work* (Ann Arbor, MI: UMI Research Press, 1985). That biography and this book are meant to complement one another, the better to serve readers and scholars of Mason and his era.

In the present book, the biographical essay is deliberately both informative and interpretive. Its subjective nature sets it apart from the more objective biography published in 1985. It is assumed that readers who use this essay, the biography, and other sources will reach conclusions at variance with mine and with one another's. With biography, there are few absolutes and no "last words." Collectively, we gain understanding by weighing varied interpretations, providing those interpretations are grounded in knowledge and sensitivity.

The Catalog of Works lists all of Mason's music publications chronologically, including a few works unobtainable for annotation. That catalog provides subtitles and publication data insofar as the information can be ascertained. Readers may also find the classified and alphabetical listings of titles helpful (pages 179 and 183 respectively).

Unlike other volumes in this series, this book does not include a discography. Recordings of Mason's anthems and children's music are non-existent, or if existent, not as commercial recordings referenced in standard sources on discography. There are some recordings of a few of Mason's most famous hymn tunes, chiefly these: Bethany ("Nearer My God To Thee"); Boylston ("A Charge to Keep I Have"); Hamburg ("When I Survey the Wondrous Cross"); Missionary Hymn ("From Greenland's Icy Mountains"); Olivet ("My Faith Looks Up To Thee"). My research led me to conclude that readers would be better served by my devoting space in this book to other kinds of information.

The Bibliography is divided into two parts: writings by Mason and writings about Mason. In preparing the annotated bibliography of writings about Mason, I faced two difficult decisions: which works to include and what to write about each one. Both decisions were difficult, but the first was the more difficult of the two. As a first step, I chose to exclude music and biographical dictionaries and music encyclopedias of our times because readers would turn to these references without suggestions from this book.

That choice left the harder question of what to include. Representative writers from Mason's day to the present seemed to warrant inclusion, thereby revealing changes in interpretation over time. Writings focused on Mason's contemporaries also deserve a place because Mason and his work need to be seen in the context of his relationships with others. It seemed proper to include writers whose specialties parallel Mason's interests (e.g., church music, music education, and music publishing), recognizing not only Mason's varied career, but also readers' varied interests. It also seemed important to include representative works of many other kinds, both biographical and bibliographical, to point readers to additional sources.

Then came the second question: what to write about each work. Being complete enough to give a fair picture of contents while remaining brief is obviously a challenge. Some of my annotations are more like abstracts, the presumption being that more information would help readers, thus justifying the space and the inconsistency in length of the annotations. Generally, older and otherwise difficult-to-obtain publications got more extensive coverage.

Annotating followed these broad guidelines, plus a few specific considerations mentioned at the opening of individual sections below. As a final word, it might be noted that no matter how carefully an author defines guidelines, annotating is highly subjective and should be interpreted as such by readers.

The frontispiece is taken from "The Great Peace Jubilee," by Sarah B. Lawrence (*New England Magazine*, 32 [1905]: 168). The date and the artist are not known. This picture was selected because it shows strength and determination written into the very lines of Mason's face by his later years, the years following controversy and accomplishment.

The picture seems just right for this book for other reasons as well. This likeness comes from an artist's conception, not from a camera. Consequently it has a subjective, interpretive quality that parallels the interpretive nature of the biographical sketch and the annotations contained in this book.

The haziness of the picture also parallels the haziness of understanding that has surrounded its subject. It is my hope that this book will help readers see through the haziness of history into the strength and determination that so characterized Lowell Mason.

Acknowledgments

This book owes a great deal to the many scholars and librarians who have assisted me during my years of research on Lowell Mason. The libraries most important for Lowell Mason material are the Yale University Music Library, the Beinecke Rare Book and Manuscript Library at Yale, the Boston Public Library, and the Boston Athenaeum.

In preparation of this book, I also explored the holdings of the Carnegie Library in Pittsburgh; the American Antiquarian Society Library, Worcester, Massachusetts; Loeb Music Library at Harvard University; the New York Public Library; and the Music Division of the Library of Congress. I am grateful to the staff members at all those libraries for their help.

I am particularly indebted to Dr. Bruce D. Wilson, Curator of the Special Collections in Music at the University of Maryland, College Park, Maryland. That collection is better known as the MENC (Music Educators National Conference) Historical Center. The resources of that collection are highly significant to a study of Lowell Mason, but in addition, Dr. Wilson is a distinguished scholar of Mason's work in Boston. His research and insights into the Boston Public Schools during Mason's years in Boston have proved invaluable to my work.

Without the help of Greenwood Press staff members, this book would never have come into existence. I am especially grateful to Marilyn Brownstein, Humanities Editor, and to Don Hixon, Series Adviser, for their skillful guidance. Lastly, I am grateful to friends and family for their patient support.

Lowell Mason

Biography

Introduction: The Making of a Legend

He arose, "stepped forward upon the platform with his easy, graceful step, an ease and grace, by the way, which marked every action of his." He spoke on teaching vocal music, and though some of his listeners were skeptical, his voice, manner, and ideas won their attention: "The effect was like an electric shock." When speaking on music teaching, this master teacher offered lessons of "great value to many a teacher, not simply as lessons on *singing*, but as lessons in *teaching*.["]1

That account was based on eyewitness observations of Lowell Mason at the height of his career. The writer had observed Mason at a teachers' institute in 1850 and at an annual meeting of the National Teachers' Association in 1865. By that time, Mason could look back upon decades of accomplishment, these among others:

- instituting curricular music in the Boston Public Schools and developing a vocal music program there;
- implementing training programs for music teachers, from brief conventions to extensive institutes, and training general classroom teachers in vocal music teaching at teachers' institutes;
- publishing dozens of tunebooks, textbooks, hymnals, sheet music, and other works, many with subsequent editions;

- teaching in public and private institutions, on the elementary, secondary, and post-secondary levels;
- conducting major choral groups in choral-society, academy, and church settings; directing music programs in major churches, and serving as organist;
- composing/arranging hundreds of hymns, anthems, psalm settings, chants, glees and other secular music, and children's music;
- rearing his family, helping his older two sons get established in music publishing, his younger two sons in instrument manufacturing and performing.

By the last twenty years of his life, Mason was also becoming a legend, i.e., a popular, somewhat romanticized figure larger than life. The word *legend* suggests distortion and half truth; yet, even half truth contains some truth. Generally, accomplishments undergird a legend, and a charismatic personality encourages legend-making. Such is the case with Mason, as revealed by contemporary observations.

Of Mason and his followers at teachers' conventions, John Sullivan Dwight commented that Mason "is the magnet, and they are all true as steel."[2] Dwight described the scene at the 1845 Teachers' Convention in Boston:

> They are his army mustered from all parts of the land; and in them he greatly delighteth; for they think there was never one...like unto him....Some you will see of a bustling character...whose enthusiasm and devotion to their general will not let them keep their seats, but they must be continually approaching him and volunteering to do his errands....We overheard one saying: "Mr. M. is the master spirit of the age"; and it looked as if he believed it; and it was not the master's fault if he did not....[3]

Chief among the accomplishments underlying the Mason legend was his success in getting music accepted into the Boston Public School curriculum in 1838. In the years that followed, school music attracted ever more people and more resources as it became established across the nation. Mason lived to see new, younger generations of music teachers, thousands of them trained in his conventions and institutes, well acquainted with his books, and well practiced in his pedagogy. His reputation grew in tandem with the music education movement.

Mason was an indefatigable promoter whose name and image were before the public for decades, partly through his tireless publishing and public speaking and partly through the actions of others. Throughout his career, he showed unusual gifts for charming, persuading, and leading others. Once charmed and persuaded, his followers expounded his ideas and spread his name yet further. Critics also spread Mason's ideas by using them as points of departure: his concepts of church music and Pestalozzian music teaching, in particular, were convenient walls against which opponents bounced their own ideas.

Admirers and detractors agreed on at least one point: Mason's career made an enormous impact on American culture. By the time of his death at age eighty, Mason had outlasted many of his critics, leaving the writing of obituaries and tributes to people who had known him only as a venerable senior figure, seemingly above struggle and controversy. Some of the accomplishments for which he was eulogized were not the accomplishments of any one person alone, but rather, the consequence of large-scale movements of the times: music in the schools, teacher training, revived congregational singing, and music publishing.

After Mason's death, his legend continued to grow. Some decades passed before the preparation of Mason's biography was undertaken, and then it was undertaken as a labor of love by one of his grandsons, Henry Lowell Mason (1864-1957). Beginning about 1909, Henry worked with devotion and care, gathering information and drafting a biography. Early in his work, Henry contacted people who had known his grandfather, asking them to share what they could recall. By so doing, he salvaged priceless memories that would otherwise have been lost. Through nearly fifty years' work, Henry producing a manuscript rich in detail, but unfinished when he died in 1957.

During Henry Lowell Mason's lifetime, other researchers were attracted to Lowell Mason material, but chose to leave the writing of a biography alone, even if they were well along with research. In the words of Mason scholar Arthur L. Rich, "When I realized how much Henry Mason had set his heart on being recognized as his grandfather's biographer, I set aside the new material I had assembled and let my book remain an educational study."[4]

After the death of Henry Lowell Mason in 1957, his heirs contributed the manuscript biography and related documents to the Yale University Library. Now in the Beinecke Rare Book and Manuscript Library, the Lowell Mason Papers reside near the Lowell Mason Library (or Collection), the latter Mason's private library of about 10,300 items, including textbooks, hymnals, tunebooks, sheet music, treatises, journals, and other works.

A detailed account of Lowell Mason's life and career was published in 1985, an account that drew upon Henry Lowell Mason's work and many other sources, including unpublished theses and dissertations and archival nineteenth-century materials.[5] All biographical data in the pages below comes from that source unless otherwise noted. Though many details remain unknown, the Mason legend can now be weighed against more of the facts.

Finding Himself: The Early Years (1792-1827)

> I spent twenty years...doing nothing save playing all manner of instru-
> ments that came within my reach....
> — Lowell Mason to Samuel F. Smith[6]

Those twenty years were the years of Mason's youth, rough-
ly 1792-1812, spent in Medfield, Massachusetts, a small town
about twenty miles southwest of Boston. Lowell Mason was
born January 8, 1792, into a family long-established in Medfield. His father, Johnson Mason, was a descendant of Robert
Mason, an English immigrant who helped settle the community
around 1650. His mother, Catherine (Caty) Hartshorn Mason,
could trace her ancestry back to English immigrants who arrived in Massachusetts in 1637 and settled in Medfield in 1651.

The Masons were a comfortable, middle-class family;
Johnson Mason was co-owner of a dry goods store. Around
1801, he and his partner began manufacturing straw bonnets, an
enterprise that soon became Medfield's leading industry. As a
young man growing up in that setting, Lowell Mason had a
stable home and community, the basic common-school education typical of the times, and religious training in the local Congregational church. The eldest in a family of five, he began early
to understand children, handle them, and assume responsibility
for them; by working with his father, he learned business practices, public relations, and management skills.

Mason's early musical training was sketchy, but he took advantage of the opportunities around him. He attended singing
schools led by Amos Albee and Oliver Shaw, learned from
practices of local musicians, and participated in local performing groups. He became director of his church choir at age 16,
and, in connection with this position, wrote his first anthem,

"Ordination," in 1812. Mason, who played the violin, cello, flute, piano, organ, and clarinet, first directed a band at about age 18. Younger than some of his players, he learned to play some of the instruments as he went along.

Despite apparent talent and enthusiasm for music, Lowell Mason could not plan to make a living as a musician. He realized that there were few opportunities for full-time professional musicians. Furthermore, although Johnson and Caty Mason encouraged their children to learn and enjoy music, like other parents of the day, they urged their children to pursue careers in more promising fields.

Undecided about a career choice, Lowell Mason went to Boston during the winter of 1810-11, looking for work and for direction in his life. Those months in Boston proved to be significant, though not in the ways he had hoped. Through a mutual friend in Medfield, Mason met Joseph Stevens Buckminster, a young clergyman who played the flute, cello, violin, and organ. As an outgrowth of his musical interests, Buckminster sought to improve singing in his church. To that end, he had prepared a tunebook for his congregation, the *Brattle Square Collection* (1810). The goal of congregational singing was unfamiliar to young Mason who had heard little such singing in his youth.

Finding neither suitable work nor any other reason to remain in Boston, Mason went back to Medfield in the spring of 1811, evidently to work again in the family business. As time passed, he saw his contemporaries settle into careers while he was still searching for his life's work. When two of his friends decided to move to the thriving city of Savannah, Georgia, in late 1812, Mason decided to go along.

Making a new life in Georgia. The trip to Savannah was hard and expensive: fifty-five days, 1088 miles by horse and wagon. When he arrived, Mason had only a few dollars and was in debt to his father for money advanced during the trip. He immediately settled into a rooming house, found a church home at the Independent Presbyterian Church, and sought work. At the church he met another Massachusetts native, dry-goods merchant Edward Stebbins, a man twenty-eight years his senior. Stebbins took an interest in the young man, hired him, and in a few years made him a partner in the firm of Stebbins & Mason.

During his first years in Savannah, while building the dry-goods business and assuming leadership in church and civic affairs, Lowell Mason appeared to replicate his father's life, though in a larger community. He proved to be a leader when he helped expand his church's Sunday school to enroll more children, irrespective of their church affiliations, and, by 1826, to include black children, a "first" in North America. He became superintendent of the Sunday school in 1815 and remained so throughout his Savannah years, a position in which he directed teachers, wrote circulars and reports, and handled discipline and budgets.

Concurrently, to earn a little more money and to indulge his musical interests, Mason ran singing schools, the first of which began about three weeks after his arrival. In January 1815 he became the choir director at his church, and a few years later, accepted the position of organist as well.

Upon arriving in Savannah, Mason wrote to his family, revealing exhaustion from the trip and discouragement: "if I make two hundred dollars in all I shall think I do well." He added that he needed at least two or three hundred dollars even to return home.[7] Yet, within a few years, his part-time work as church musician alone brought twice that amount. By 1820 the church owed him $650, a debt incurred because available funds were absorbed by a building program undertaken in 1817. Mason went on leading the music program, assuming (correctly) that the church would pay him as soon as possible.

The move to Savannah proved to Mason that he could establish himself in an unfamiliar environment. He proved to be a skilled businessman who, with his partner, built a flourishing business. Even so, that business did not survive the death of his partner in 1819 or 1820, forcing another change of direction. At that time, Mason became a clerk at Planter's Bank, a position he held as long as he remained in Savannah. In the early years in Savannah, Mason had also shown unusual ability to make friends and allies, winning their support for his ideas.

Preparing for his career.   During his Savannah years, Mason compiled a tunebook that launched his career: *The Boston Handel and Haydn Society Collection of Church Music.* Throughout its twenty-two editions, that book inspired and subsidized his other work, including gratuitous teaching and public speaking and meagerly paid church work. The book was an extraordinary success, winning acclaim in this country and in England: this book "is a work, containing one of the most complete collections of psalmody that ever was embodied. It demonstrates the advancement of the Americans in music..."[8]

In retrospect, it is apparent that the publication of that tunebook had more impact on Mason's subsequent career than any other single experience of the Savannah years. But as Mason was living through those years, he could not have foreseen its impact. Nor could he have foreseen the value of the many skills he was developing during those years, skills upon which his later career came to depend: not just performing, conducting, composing, and arranging; but also public speaking, writing, and editing; teaching and leading other teachers. All the while, Mason was also developing friendships with musicians and non-musicians, including some relationships that lasted a lifetime.

While in Savannah, Mason steadily built his reputation as a church musician. On May 9, 1819, for instance, the music he conducted at dedication ceremonies for the new church won praise as "peculiarly well adapted to the solemnity of the occasion," tending to "elevate the soul to sublime and heavenly musings."[9] President James Monroe happened to be present on that occasion. Over the years, Mason's church work was much observed and reported upon; his choirs presented well-received public concerts that were favorably reviewed in Savannah papers. His work became known for its excellence, both in organization and in musicianship.

Soon after settling in Savannah, Mason began studying figured bass through correspondence with Boston organist S. P. Taylor. A few years later he hired Frederick Abel, a talented German immigrant, to be his private tutor. Abel led Mason into composition and arranging, encouraging him to compile his own music book. Mason patterned his collection of hymn and psalm tunes after a popular English collection, William Gardiner's *Sacred Melodies from Haydn, Mozart and Beethoven, Adapted to the Best English Poets and Appropriated to the Use of the British Church*, published in two volumes in England (1812, 1815) with American printings beginning in 1818.

Launching his career. By the early 1820s, Mason was searching for a publisher for his music collection. His friendship with church musician Thomas Hastings (1784-1872), a relationship based on mutual esteem as well as common interests, dates from the same period; the two men shared and compared ideas about church music through letter writing. Hastings' support for his concepts must have been heartening to Mason as he sought a publisher, first in Savannah, then in Philadelphia and Boston. For a time, he had no success, though he sought no royalties.

Finally, at the suggestion of William Goodrich, a Boston organ builder who installed a new instrument in the Savannah church, Mason went to Boston in person to seek a publisher. From the standpoint of his career, Mason's trip to Boston served him well. As often happened in his career, Mason won the backing of a prominent person and organization and subsequently enjoyed success beyond his expectations.

In the case of his first tunebook, Mason sought the backing of Dr. George K. Jackson, organist of the Boston Handel and Haydn Society. Jackson, an eccentric but accomplished musician, approved publication, and within five days Mason and the society entered into the first of many contracts. Though Mason's name did not appear on the title page until the ninth edition, his role was widely known through remarks in the book's preface and in the media.

The publication of this tunebook altered the course of Mason's life in three ways. First, he caught a glimpse of his future in publishing. It was evident almost from the moment of publication that his musical ideas were acceptable to others, as measured by critical review and by book sales. Those sales demonstrated to Mason that he could make money as a tunebook compiler; the success of his book insured financial stability for the society for decades and added substantially to Mason's comfort as well. It inspired further compiling and editing, work he continued throughout his life with immense professional and financial success.

Second, with the success of the tunebook, Mason became a prominent member of the Boston Handel and Haydn Society overnight, prominence that led to his election as president a few years later. Mason maintained his ties with the organization for the rest of his life. The society's goals were in harmony with Mason's goals: first-rate performances of choral masterworks for American audiences and publication of choral music for Americans' use.

Third, the fact that his book was published in Boston held special significance for Mason. That city had a powerful appeal, and not just because of its cultural, educational, and religious leadership. No matter how impressive his successes in Georgia, Massachusetts was "home." On September 3, 1817, he had married Abigail (Abby) Gregory of Westborough, Massachusetts, and though she, too, adjusted to Savannah, she longed for "home." After their first two sons were born, the Masons thought even more about educational advantages "back home." In a letter to her mother, Abby admitted that "the moment we can see any reasonable prospect of obtaining a decent and comfortable support at the North...we will give up the pecuniary advantages of the South—and return with gladness and thankfulness to the hills of...Massachusetts."[10]

Becoming a public figure in Boston. With his book of church music selling well, Mason traveled to Boston and presented a major public address on church music in October 1826. His reputation, both as a tunebook author and as a practicing church musician, gave credence to his statements on the role of church music and the need for its reform. That address was published, thereby putting his name and ideas before an ever-widening audience. The experience also revealed to him another dimension of his abilities: the ability to move audiences through public speaking.

As one consequence of that address, a committee comprised of representatives from three Boston churches organized to hire Mason as music director in their churches. Between December 1826 and April 1827, the committee offered him three successive contracts, each of which he turned down, not-withstanding the attractions of moving to Boston and the chance to expand his work with church music.

During the summer of 1827, plans changed abruptly, and in August the Masons moved to Boston. Whatever reluctance Mason had felt suddenly evaporated, and he negotiated with the churches at once. From all indications, he changed his mind because he learned that the Handel and Haydn Society would elect a new president in September; Amasa Winchester, having served the society for seven years, declined to continue. Only after Mason heard of Winchester's decision did he seriously consider moving to Boston; then, having made the decision, he moved at once.

As he expected, Mason was elected president of the Boston Handel and Haydn Society in September 1827. He served in that capacity for five years, building the organization and con-ducting major works, including Haydn's *Creation*, Handel's *Messiah*, and America's premier performance of Haydn's *Mass in B Flat* (January 18, 1829).[11] Almost from the start, he coached singers in extra sessions outside rehearsal time, a prac-tice that foreshadowed his achievements in music education and paralleled his work with Boston church choirs.

The contract between Mason and the Boston churches guaranteed him $2,000 salary for eighteen months' work, direct-ing music programs at three churches for successive periods of six months each: Hanover Street Church with clergyman Lyman Beecher; Essex Street Church with Samuel Green; and Park Street Church with Edward Beecher. Working with leading clergy must have been another attraction from Mason's standpoint, given his devotion to the church.[12]

Establishing a Career: The Boston Years (1827-1851)

> I am fully convinced that we need a reformation in the music of the Church....But how shall this reformation be brought about? Musical knowledge must be extended, and attention of the people must be called to the subject....If we could have a man well qualified who would...do something practical in the way of enlightening and leading taste, great good might be expected to result.
> —Lowell Mason, in a letter to Austin Willey, June 27, 1838[13]

Cultivating church music. Lowell Mason worked all his life to improve church music, and to that end, he worked as tirelessly in Boston as he had in Savannah. During the Boston years, he published about seventy separate publications, approximately fifty of which contained sacred music. He taught without pay at Andover Theological Seminary for eight years (1836-1844), enriching the musical background of prospective clergy. Throughout the Boston years, he served as an organist and choir director, handling music programs of major churches.

Mason's church work in Boston began under the terms negotiated with the three Boston churches, and his musical leadership more than fulfilled their expectations. Mason remained at the Park Street Church for two years beyond the six months specified by contract. While there, in 1829, he became the first organist in the history of that church; in 1830, he conducted one of the first American public performances of a children's choir, if not *the* first. A more famous "first" at the Park Street Church was the July 4, 1831, premier performance of "America," with Samuel F. Smith's text "My Country, 'Tis of Thee."

To build his church choirs, Mason began children's classes in 1828. By 1830 he was teaching 150 to 200 children at the Park Street Church, tuition free, provided they agreed to remain for the entire year. Though he was teaching music reading and singing ostensibly to develop his church choirs, he was also honing his teaching skills and building his reputation as a gifted teacher.

Absorbing cultural influences. The climate was right for teaching and for music. New England had led the nation educationally for years, and in the early 1800s, expanded educational opportunities yet further. Boston, in particular, led the way in educational and cultural expansion.

One evidence of Boston's leadership was the forming of an organization called the American Institute of Instruction. Begun locally in March 1830, the institute drew about three hundred representatives from eleven states to its first gathering in August 1830. The institute, a major influence on education for decades, worked to improve public education by extending the curriculum beyond "the three R's" and by upgrading school facilities and teaching methods. For many years, the institute sponsored regional gatherings of educators and promoted educational improvements through publications.[14]

Lowell Mason's move to Boston came at the very time when the climate favored such organizations as the American Institute for Instruction. The Boston Handel and Haydn Society had developed in 1815 from that same climate. An outgrowth of the Park Street Church choir and concerts celebrating the end of the War of 1812, the society undertook impressive programs that enjoyed considerable community support.

In Boston's stimulating environment, Mason met associates whose influence molded his career. One was George J. Webb (1803-1887), an accomplished English musician who emigrated in 1830. Mason and Webb, who met through the Handel and Haydn Society, came to share teaching and editing responsibilities for many years. The extent of Mason's dependency on Webb's formal knowledge of music can only be imagined; at the very least, it must have equaled Mason's dependence on another Boston acquaintance, William C. Woodbridge (1794-1845), whose ideas shaped Mason's pedagogy. Woodbridge was the clergyman, teacher, and writer through whom Mason became acquainted with the educational theories of Johann Heinrich Pestalozzi (1746-1827) and his followers.

The stimulation of men like Webb and Woodbridge was a major advantage for Mason during his first years in Boston. Lacking in formal education, Mason constantly read, studied, listened, and learned from musicians, educators, and others whose formal education surpassed his own. Mason's lifelong learning was described by A. W. Thayer years later:

> If you should ever go into his [Mason's] library, you will see there at a glance to what his success has been due. You will find that whatever came from the press bearing upon sacred music and the science of teaching it, found its way at once to his study; and the notes and marks in books and periodicals prove how carefully all were perused... [15]

Mason heard Woodbridge advocate teaching methods unfamiliar to him. Woodbridge was a persuasive orator, but because his own methods brought results, Mason saw no need to change his ways. Music teacher Elam Ives, Jr. (1802-1864), of Hartford, Connecticut, had experimented with the new approach, called "Pestalozzian" by Woodbridge, and in 1832 published a textbook, *American Elementary Singing Book* using the new pedagogy. Mason listened and watched, apparently with curiosity but detachment.

Adopting a pedagogy. Perhaps more attractive to Mason than specific strategies of the Pestalozzian approach was the emphasis upon offering music instruction to *all* school children because it would inculcate "habits of order and obedience." [16] Woodbridge argued along those lines at the American Institute of Instruction in his speech, "On Vocal Music as a Branch of Common Education," on August 19, 1830. Mason must have agreed with Woodbridge about the need for broadly based music teaching; indeed, in his address of 1826, he had advocated the very same thing as essential to the reform of church music.

In the months that followed, Woodbridge persuaded Mason to try Pestalozzian methods. More to his own amazement than Woodbridge's, Mason was convinced and thereafter promoted precepts he attributed to Pestalozzi, including these:

- teach things (experiences) first, signs (symbols) later;
- base teaching on an understanding of the children;
- promote wholesome mental and spiritual growth;
- lead children to think for themselves, to rely on their mental powers, and to use their curiosity.

Mason also correlated religion and Pestalozzian teaching: the method is "no other than the spirit of the gospel, applied to the work of education."[17]

Mason's teaching expanded rapidly in the early 1830s, both in numbers of students reached and in types of classes. In addition to the children's classes run in churches, he taught in private schools in Boston and experimented with music classes for the blind at the Perkins Institute for the Blind from 1832 to 1836. Still other teaching opportunities opened up with the creation of the Boston Academy of Music in January 1833.

Establishing a base. The Boston Academy of Music began as an association of about fifty business, professional, and political leaders who sought to extend more and better music opportunities to the community. Though Mason was the principal figure in the academy, he remained purposely in the background, assuming only the title "Professor," while prominent civic leaders served as academy officers. His years as a business and civic leader in Savannah must have added to Mason's credibility in the sight of Boston's business and civic community; Mason knew how to think and act like one of them because he *was* one of them, perhaps to a greater extent than either he or they realized.

Mason and the academy had identical goals and practices. With George J. Webb as the other principal professor, the academy ran individual and group lessons, vocal and instrumental, in and around Boston; established performing choral and instrumental groups; presented public concerts, lectures, teachers' conventions; published books, music, and a music magazine; and promoted the adoption of music into the public school curriculum.

The Boston Academy of Music immediately drew large numbers of students: during the first six months alone, 1500 pupils; during the second year, over 3,000.[18] Academy choirs, involving hundreds of voices, developed into major performing groups. During the 1840s, instrumental concerts were added to the academy's public performances, an addition well received in the community. Though many academy concerts included both vocal and instrumental works, they soon featured major orchestra works, such as the first American performances of Beethoven symphonies in 1841-1842.

Training teachers.   The academy pioneered in teacher training by holding annual conventions of a week to ten days' duration. These gatherings provided lectures and demonstrations on music teaching plus choral rehearsals and performances. The first convention, held in 1834, was attended by only twelve teachers, but the number more than doubled to twenty-eight in two years. Each year enrollment increased, often dramatically. By the 1840s, the conventions enrolled hundreds of teachers, evidence of the need for such instruction and the receptivity toward it.[19]

Mason and Webb organized, promoted, and led the teachers' conventions year after year. In 1841, following a "falling out" with Mason, Webb ran a convention under the auspices of the Boston Handel and Haydn Society. The rift between the two men was soon mended, and Webb resumed working with Mason at the academy. Mason and Webb provided lectures, demonstrations, and music for the conventions, based upon their teaching experience and (as years passed) their proliferating texts and tunebooks.

Facing critics. In some instances, Mason and his associates had differences that led to lasting bitterness, part of it an outgrowth of frictions that developed in the conventions and part of it an outgrowth of mid-1840s politics in the Boston Public Schools. Feelings became intense. During the August 1846 music teachers' convention, Mason, who was on the platform, saw his critic H.W. Day in the audience. Mason picked up a Bible and read, "Now there was a day when the sons of God came together, and Satan also came among them." With that, he shut the book, marched down the aisle, and walked Day out of the hall.[20]

During those years, Mason's most vocal critics were H. W. Day and George Washington Lucas, both of them former Mason associates and friends. Day and Lucas, who had became friends, joined in denouncing Mason's management of the conventions. Day also accused Mason of favoritism in selecting music teachers for the schools, and Lucas (among other criticisms) described Mason's academy teaching to be inadequate and his publishing motives to be purely mercenary:

....As a general thing, the graduates of the "Boston Academy of Music" have been found utterly incompetent to teach church music and this has led many to disregard the whole subject....In all his Choirs, Teachers' Classes, and Musical Conventions, he [Mason] has ever been...the centre [*sic*] and radiation of the most consummate cant, quackery and self-display. He speaks of "emotion." Cool, cunning, and selfish, what music ever moistened his eye, or except the clinking of silver and gold, ever touched his heart?[21]

Silver and gold were "clinking" in the sense that, by the mid-1840s, Mason's books had already made him a modest fortune, and the end of his amassing wealth was nowhere in sight. With each passing year, previous works generated more royalties, and more books rolled off the printing presses. The impact of this largely unexpected wealth on Mason's career and his thinking have been little examined; indeed, the fortune he made has been noted, but only in passing — except by rival book compilers of his day.

The teachers' conventions were tied into money-making through book sales. Those who ran conventions (whether Mason or others) promoted their books and their pedagogy. Normally the pedagogy and the books fit together as a package presented to teachers, often resulting in teachers being sold on both the ideas and the books. At the same time, the teachers' conventions served broader purposes; they were useful to participants, most of whom had few opportunities for gaining information and developing collegiality.

Eventually the conventions led to institutes and choral festivals, but from the beginning, there were immediate consequences. First, they spread Mason's pedagogical ideas into the many states represented at the conventions. The pedagogy taught at the conventions was spelled out in the *Manual of the Boston Academy of Music* (1834), a work based upon a book by Stuttgart music teacher G.F. Kübler with adaptation by Mason. Second, the conventions, by drawing so many educators from many communities, demonstrated widespread support for music in the schools, thus making a political statement.

Promoting school music. The academy promoted music teaching in the public schools not only through the teachers' conventions, but also through many other means. Academy professors proved the effectiveness of music teaching by conducting successful private school classes and singing schools throughout the Boston area. Children's classes from the academy itself performed publicly as demonstration groups, underscoring points made in speeches favoring school music.

Meanwhile, the academy encouraged community leaders, among them political leaders and the clergy, to speak and work for music in the schools. From July 1835 to June 1836, the academy also published a music magazine, *The Musical Library*, one purpose for which was editorializing for music in the schools. Books and magazines, public addresses and private contacts, convention and concerts—through all the media, the same message was proclaimed: music is important for people young and old and should be readily available to all, beginning with all school children.

Although the city of Boston was more amenable to that message—indeed, to all the goals the academy represented—than other cities would have been at the time, the idea of music in the public school curriculum met strong resistance. Many people argued that musical talent was too rare to justify teaching music to all children; that music would undermine discipline; that music was not practical; that music would waste precious time; and that adding music to the curriculum would open the door to other "frivolous" subjects.

To overcome such objections, speech-making alone was not sufficient, no matter the eloquence of music education spokesmen. Solid evidence of successful teaching in the form of children's performances was not sufficient either, despite their electrifying effect on skeptical audiences. The fact that growing numbers of teachers from many states convened in Boston annually, specifically to study music and music teaching, made a powerful political statement about growing, widespread support for music teaching, and yet, that statement did not overcome resistance either.

Building toward August 28, 1838. No single factor brought music into the schools of Boston, but rather, a combination. During the early 1830s, music in the primary schools was studied and authorized, but not implemented. The Snelling Report of 1832, central to the primary-school music initiative, was nonetheless important as a step toward later events.[22]

In 1836-37, citizens petitioned the Boston School Committee to include music in the grammar schools. These petitions were set aside until January 1837 when Samuel A. Eliot became mayor of Boston and, by virtue of that office, head of the School Committee. As one of his first acts, he established a study committee to examine the desirability of music in the schools. Led by attorney T. Kemper Davis, the three-member committee conducted a thorough study, including queries sent to administrators in private schools where music had been offered to students.

The Davis Committee Report, presented to the School Committee on August 24, 1837, endorsed music in the schools with resounding, reasoned support.[23] Acting on that report at their September 19 meeting, the School Committee authorized music classes in four grammar schools during 1837-38 as an experiment. The classes were to be run under the auspices of the Boston Academy of Music.

While the Davis report was being prepared, Lowell Mason began his first trip to Europe, a trip that began April 25 and ended November 1, 1837. In Europe he attended concerts and church services, observed music teaching in Swiss and German schools, gathered ideas and materials for use in America, and formed friendships with European educators and musicians. According to his travel diaries and letters, Mason was warmly received into the private company of educators, composers, performers, and publishers; his reputation as a church musician, tunebook compiler, and music educator had preceded him.

During the fall of 1837, while Mason was still traveling in Europe, the Boston City Council debated the authorization for music instruction in the four grammar schools, then refused to provide funding. Music in the schools became a heated public controversy with pro's and con's argued in the newspapers.[24] The goal so long hoped for—seemingly so near at hand—seemed to be slipping away by default.

When Lowell Mason returned from Europe on November 1, 1837, and learned about recent developments, he volunteered to teach without salary and to supply the materials himself. On November 14, 1837, the School Committee accepted his offer, specifying that he would teach in one school, Hawes Grammar School in South Boston. His work would be observed not only by Hawes administrators and faculty, but also by a music committee charged with quarterly reporting to the School Committee.

Fulfilling hopes. In December 1837, Mason began teaching at Hawes School. Because separation by gender was customary at the time, Mason ran identical twice-a-week classes, thirty minutes each, one for boys and one for girls. The children ranged in age from about eight to fourteen. Hawes School was a good choice for the experiment in that few of the children had prior or concurrent music training, and their parents and Hawes administrators were supportive of the experiment. Quarterly reports to the School Committee indicate that the children were attentive, participated gladly, and learned their music lessons well.

In schools at that time, summer vacation amounted to only a few weeks in late August. The 1837-38 year for Hawes School ended with a demonstration program on August 14, 1838, showing the children's accomplishments in music and other subjects. Mason selected eight songs for the occasion, seven of them from his *Juvenile Singing School* (compiled with Webb, 1837), the eighth published later in *The Boston School Song Book* (1841). The program opened with "Flowers, Wildwood Flowers," the first piece sung by American public school children as part of an official school program.

The success of the Hawes School experiment and the impact of the August 14 program influenced School Committee deliberations in the days that followed, as did the enthusiastic endorsements of Hawes School Principal Joseph Harrington, Jr. and the music committee. Speaking before the American Institute of Instruction, Harrington used what he had seen and heard during the experimental year as the basis for supporting school music:

> Is it *practicable* to introduce vocal music into schools? — The most conclusive answer...I could make to this question would be, "go and see." The experiment has been tried, and one successful experiment is worth a thousand theoretical refutations....Such then, is one fact; — and testimony of this kind might be indefinitely accumulated....Is not one school, selected at random, a fair representative of the whole? What is true of human capability in Boston, is true of human capability in Lowell, and in every town in the Commonwealth. [25]

Others were asking the same questions at the same time. The 1838 teachers' convention at the Boston Academy of

Music, representing nine states and the District of Columbia, met in August 1838. After debating the merits of vocal music as a branch of public school education, members passed a resolution supporting school music. That vote was taken August 21, 1838, as a climax to the convention. Though the 138 convention members returned to their home communities, they must have been eager for news from Boston in the days that followed.

And news there was—news of historic significance. On August 28, 1838, the Boston School Committee again addressed the question of music in the schools, but on this day, the matter was settled with the passage of a long-awaited resolution. It read in part as follows:

> *Resolved,* That the Committee on Music be instructed to contract with a teacher of vocal music in the several public schools of the city.

> *Resolved,* That the instruction...shall commence in the several public schools whenever the subcommittees of the several schools...shall determine....[26]

Working in the Boston Schools. Lowell Mason was the first music teacher hired under this resolution. He had the authority to teach the classes himself or to hire assistants; he could buy the materials needed for music classes within given allocations. The first year (1838-39) he hired only one assistant, but more were added steadily so that by 1844-45, for instance, he taught in six schools without assistance and supervised ten assistants in other schools.

In September 1845, Mason was abruptly replaced as music master in the Boston schools. Despite requests for an explanation and investigation, little official action was taken. Then, in February 1846, he was partially reinstated, again with little explanation. From that point until he left the Boston school system, Mason shared his supervisory responsibilities equally with Benjamin Baker.

Though some of the factors behind the 1845-46 episode remain unknown, Mason's personal conduct and teaching skill were not issues. From his standpoint, the Boston school position was but one of many duties absorbing his energy in the 1840s: editing and publishing alone could have occupied him full-time, but he continued with teaching and other academy duties, lecturing at conventions and teachers' institutes, and heading church music programs.

Finishing the Boston years. In 1845, Lowell Mason joined the staff of the Horace Mann Institutes for Teachers. Mann had heard Mason speak before the American Institute of Instruction and admired both his methodology and his manner of presentation. Institute attendees were teachers who had little opportunity elsewhere for learning the art of teaching. Working with Horace Mann was an honor Mason never forgot. Though the institutes entailed a grueling schedule of travel, bringing inconvenience and exhaustion, Mann's pioneering to improve teacher training so appealed to Mason that he gladly participated and continued to do so, long after Horace Mann left his position in 1848.[27]

By the mid-1840s, Mason evidently had retirement on his mind. During that decade, he gradually relinquished ties that had been important to him, such as his teaching at Andover Seminary. His uncertainty about staying in Boston became apparent during contract negotiations with Central Church late in 1843. The contract as finally agreed upon included the assurances Mason sought. A letter dated December 16, 1843, read in part, "Having received your answer accepting our proposal with the condition that your removal from New England should terminate the engagement, we hereby assent to the condition."[28]

Central Church was a fitting climax for Mason's church work in Boston, given the exceptional facilities and the performing capabilities of the choir. At that church, Mason played a recently installed three-manual Appleton organ positioned so that he sat in the midst of his one-hundred voice choir. As had been his practice, he held frequent, rigorous rehearsals, including sectional rehearsals.

At Central Church, as in so many previous positions, Mason grew professionally through continuous musical practice as a performer and a conductor/teacher. Through building his choirs into fine performance groups and through extensive arranging and editing, he pursued to the last day the ideals that had taken him to Boston twenty-four years earlier.

Completing His Mission: The Final Years (1851-1872)

> That all the people might enter fully and heartily into the use and enjoyment of music in the praise of God was a paramount object of my father's life, and he believed this could be realized only as the churches should become enlightened as to the best religious use of music...
>
> — Lowell Mason, Jr., March 15, 1873[29]

Enlightening the churches "as to the best religious use of music" was Mason's primary objective during his last years. But before undertaking those final, productive years, Lowell and Abigail Mason took the first extended vacation of their lives, a sixteen-month trip to Europe and England, from December 1851 to April 1853.

Highlights of the European trip of 1852-53 are described in Mason's *Musical Letters from Abroad* (B7), a collection of fifty-four informal essays reflecting on people, places, and musical styles. The trip was extended by about six months when Mason was asked to lecture on church music and music teaching in England, specifically to encourage congregational singing in the churches.

Mason's efforts to enhance church music focused increasingly on more and better congregational singing. To that end, he advocated a musical style typical churchgoers could manage. As summarized by George Blagdon Bacon, Mason's minister and friend in Orange, New Jersey, Mason's positions were these:

- that the tunes used in the churches should be such that all could sing them;
- that the music should be a fit and natural expression of the words.[30]

To encourage more participation, Mason experimented with placing six precentors throughout the sanctuary during his brief tenure as music director at the Fifth Avenue Presbyterian Church in New York City, a position he held from May 1853 until his move to Orange, New Jersey, in late 1854.[31] Over the years, Mason also advocated chanting and published chants in many of his books. Whether with respect to chanting, hymn singing, or musical practices within churches, his goals were constant: congregational participation and text expression that enhanced worship.

Mason has been criticized for promoting European music over indigenous American music, for sweeping away a home-grown tradition with vitality and character of its own, and for free-wheeling use of the music of others. There is no doubt that Mason set out to replace music he considered inappropriate (such as the American fuguing tunes common during his youth) with music he considered appropriate, nor is there any doubt that he was a tireless arranger of the works of others. Given his purposes, the absence of applicable international copyright laws, and the endemic plagiarism of the era, his practices are understandable (though indefensible by twentieth-century standards). A man of his times in this and other respects, Mason followed the practices common in his day; had those practices been different, Lowell Mason would have been quick to do otherwise.

On many occasions, Mason defended his arranging of others' works, as in this excerpt from a letter dated February 26, 1860:

> I am much dependent upon the good German writers – among whose works I find an exhaustless store of beautiful pieces – which are already – or may be by a little arrangement adapted to the wants of our people....Now in doing this work, I fully believe that I am doing good, vastly more so, than as if I was composing myself. There are some people, who seem not to care what others have done – they ignore all that has gone before, and depend upon what they can do. I would not be so – I would rather go out of myself....I do not work for mere money – I do really desire to do that which shall improve my fellowmen... [32]

In short, Mason's preferences and practices were not based on anti-American or pro-European biases (though he lived in a cultural climate which featured the latter); but rather, Mason's preferences grew from a pragmatic view of the capacities of American singers and, so far as sacred music was concerned, his own religious convictions. He promoted music and musical practices that fit his standards; to do so, he synthesized musical ideas he found in many sources. It may be "that Mason's music is typically American in that it represents an American vernacular response to the mainstream of Western musical culture up to and including his lifetime."[33]

Publishing church music. Elements of the musical style Mason used and advocated include the following:

- diatonic melodies, kept within a moderate range;
- simple rhythms with mild syncopation, if any;
- diatonic harmony in major keys with few sharps or flats; reliance on primary chords with occasional secondary dominants;
- symmetrical phrases (generally), with repetition;
- syllabic settings; chordal style;
- singable texts, upholding the highest standards of purity in thought.

Mason was a prolific editor, producing new books and revised books constantly, as the Catalog of Works below attests. Though his composing and arranging was extensive, no one knows exactly how many tunes of his own creation appeared; many times he published his own works anonymously.[34] Henry Lowell Mason concluded that his grandfather produced 1,697 hymn tunes, 1,210 of them original, and 487 arrangements, totals somewhat disputed by later research.[35]

About the number and popularity of Mason's books, there is no dispute. His fortune made through publishing is suggested by these conservatively estimated sales figures:

Carmina Sacra and its revision, The New Carmina Sacra: at least 500,000 copies from 1841-1858

The Hallelujah: 150,000 copies from 1854-1858

All of the following sold over 50,000 copies from date of publication through 1858:

The Boston Handel and Haydn Society Collection of Church Music (1822)

The Choir (1832)

The Boston Academy's Collection of Church Music (1835)

The Modern Psalmist (1839)

The Psaltery (1845)

The National Psalmist (1848)

Cantica Laudis (1859)

Many other books sold over 10,000 copies.[36] These sales figures account for the fortune Mason amassed. His net worth upon leaving Boston in 1851 was estimated at $100,000, the equivalent of about $1,858,000 in 1986 purchasing power,[37] and his career as an editor/compiler of books was by no means finished in 1851.

Building a music library. Considering their wealth by the 1850s, the Masons were comparatively frugal, but when it came to his library, Mason spared no expense. During his trips to Europe, he purchased music constantly, including the entire private library of Johann Christian Heinrich Rinck (1770-1846), a collection of about 830 manuscripts and 700 volumes of hymnology, with rare items among them. With no hesitation, Mason purchased the entire library, thinking of its use in America by those whose musical scholarship would surpass his own:

> The lover of music and its progress among us will be glad to know that it is already packed, and will be on its way to America in a few days....There are now many young men who are beginning to feel the necessity of a more liberal education for the profession of music than has hitherto been supposed important.[38]

Mason drew upon his library constantly for his writing and editing, and he also allowed others to use it. One of the most famous visitors to his library was A.W. Thayer, whose

Beethoven research Mason supported fully. Mason underwrote some of Thayer's research, letting Thayer repay the loan at his convenience. The Mason library grew into one of the finest music libraries in the country at the time and was recognized as such in *Dwight's Journal of Music* in September 1854.[39]

Crowning efforts. When Mason returned from his 1852-53 European trip, an exciting new opportunity opened up for training music teachers. Under the leadership of George F. Root, William B. Bradbury, Thomas Hastings, and others of the "Mason circle," teachers' institutes of three months' duration began, at first under the name "New York Normal Musical Institute."

Institute sessions offered the most extensive music-teacher training of the day. Lecture topics included teaching, harmony and composition, sacred and secular music, vocal cultivation, musical taste, music history, and elocution. Private and class lessons in voice and instruments were also offered. After the first institute (summer 1853), the offerings expanded into successive three-month periods, filling the year's calendar.[40]

The New York Normal Musical Institute may well have been, as John Sullivan Dwight wrote, Mason's "crowning effort, to concentrate and build up into some distinct form of permanency the results and methods of his extensive and in many respects original experience."[41] Mason's role in the institutes was both honorary and participatory: his famous name brought stature to the institutes; his years of experience and knowledge of teaching went into lectures.

In 1856, the normal musical institute moved to North Reading, Massachusetts, at Root's instigation. There the institutes continued with an expanded faculty, including George J. Webb and William W. Killip (b. 1832). The institutes drew thousands of participants over the years and thousands more in audiences that got "their first and never-fading impressions of the glorious power and beauty of a chorus of Handel, sung by a thousand voices with orchestral and organ accompaniment."[42]

Like the conventions in earlier years, the institutes spread across the nation. Until he was about seventy years old, Mason continued to travel to institutes, some of them as far away from his home as Ohio and Missouri. Until at least age seventy-five, he also enjoyed visiting schools. From one part of the country to another, he was welcomed as a venerable figure, a patriarch of music and music education.

Seeing fruition. The last years of Mason's life were rewarding both personally and professionally. His retirement home in Orange, New Jersey, was built on a seventy-acre wooded estate about fifteen miles outside New York City. A second house was built there for the Daniel Gregory Mason (the Masons' eldest son) and his family. The other sons lived nearby, with the exception of Henry who settled in Boston. For Mason, who loved children intensely all his life, grandchildren were a great joy. The satisfaction of seeing his sons settled was also a reward: the older sons in publishing at Mason & Law and later Mason Brothers; Henry in instrument manufacturing in the firm of Mason & Hamlin; William in his career as a concert pianist.

In 1854-55 Mason taught sacred music at Union Theological Seminary in New York City. The knowledge which had carried him to that position was recognized with an honorary doctorate from New York University in 1855. Even in those years of retirement, he was never far from learning and teaching.

Almost to the very end of his life, he continued working in his library, pouring over his books and music. His last publication, *The Pestalozzian Music Teacher* (1871), took longer than necessary because, as his co-editor Theodore F. Seward remarked, Mason had such a good time doing the work.[43] During his last years, Mason also worked on a harmony textbook. Copyrighted in his own name in 1868, the project later became a joint effort between Lowell and his son William. The manuscript, much of it in Lowell Mason's hand, was left unfinished when he died.

Lowell Mason enjoyed many tributes and honors during his last years. By all indications, he was at peace with himself and his world. Among the special occasions of those years were the Masons' golden wedding anniversary, celebrated at their home on September 3, 1867, and the 1869 National Peace Jubilee in Boston under Patrick S. Gilmore (1829-1892). Mason was an honored guest at that jubilee, a celebration that his career had helped make possible:

> ....all that New England has accomplished in choral music goes back for its origin to the earlier labors of Lowell Mason. He was the founder of a school, held little in esteem among the professors and students of the Italian and German methods. But it is a school that has filled New England with the singers that piled the Coliseum with the most wonderful chorus the world has ever seen; and it has laid, in thousands and tens of thousands, the foundations of a musical knowledge that has grown up to embrace an appreciation of all that is good and noble and elevating in the music of the Old World... [44]

Mason's final statements about music would seem to be those found in the draft of his proposed harmony textbook. That manuscript ends with a chapter entitled "Closing Remarks." The chapter, written entirely in Mason's hand, opens with his comment that the content is "subject to the alterations and additions of the Junior editor." The junior editor (William Mason) left the draft virtually untouched.

These paragraphs, taken from the end of his drafted "Closing Remarks," summarize his views and his hopes for the future:

> It is pleasing to look back for a quarter or half a century and retrace the wonderful and very rapid progress which has been made in the art both of vocal and instrumental music during that time. This is to be attributed in no small degree to German immigration, and to German skill and general musical influence. It is also a source of high gratification to know that in many parts of our country there are not a few young Americans, who having, many of them, received a thorough education, at home or abroad, do now greatly increase and strengthen the ranks of advance in true musical art and science.

> May the future progress of music in this land be so directed and controlled as to insure its important aid to the highest degree of human culture, and thus to the attainment of a higher and more enduring happiness than that of the mere sensuous gratification which its performance does not fail immediately to afford. May its refining and elevating influence be experienced in private, in the family, in school, in social life, and may the house of worship be made to resound with the chorus of universal praise.[45]

Conclusion: Seeing the Man Behind the Legend

> Goodness is more to be desired than greatness.
> — Lowell Mason, Preface, iii, *Mason's Normal Singer* (1856)

Lowell Mason died peacefully in his home on August 11, 1872, at the age of 80. The funeral was held August 15 at the Orange Valley Congregational Church with burial at Rosedale Cemetery. Praise poured forth in the press, but had he been asked, he would more likely have chosen to be remembered not only in terms of professional accomplishment, but in terms of the personal qualities he meant by "goodness."

The goodness in which Lowell Mason believed and which he tried to exemplify was based on lifelong trust in human capability and malleability and on lifelong faith in God. He trusted others almost to the point of being naive: he believed in those who seemed to agree with him and never quite understood why they might turn on him. But there were many sides to his personality, and at times, he was harsh with associates, expressing anger and bitterness.

Mason's generosity was widely exercised and widely recognized: "his wealth...would have been far greater, were his benevolence less."[46] Even his critics knew they could rely on his benevolence, as did the broken and beggarly George Washington Lucas, very near the end of Mason's life.[47] Mason was, in short, a basically good and earnest man, a steward of his abilities; steeped in the Protestant work ethic, he was "a workman who needeth not to be ashamed."

Nevertheless, his successes were due to more than innate goodness; those successes owed much to his rare talents for dealing with others — non-musicians as well as musicians — and to his sensitivity and adaptability to public opinion and climate. Ever sure of his purposes and his abilities, he was adept at developing the right alliances at the right times and the right places, all serving the objectives to which he was committed.

The Lowell Mason legend grew because it embodies purposes larger than a single life: namely, bringing music into the lives of Americans young and old, in churches, schools, and communities — wherever they are, by whatever means is appropriate. At the time of Mason's death, his contemporaries reflected on his impact upon American life. Perhaps we can do no better today than to consider Lowell Mason — the man, his legend, and his legacy — as he was seen then:

> We announced, yesterday, the death of a man who has, during a long life, exercised an extraordinary influence upon the educational interests of New England and of the country at large. For forty-five years,

Mr. Mason has been the head and front of popular music education in this country....One generation after another...have learned to read and sing the music that he has composed and printed, and his name has come down from father to son, from mother to daughter, as the chief apostle of a popular system of a branch of education...

His personal contributions to sacred music, principally in the form of hymn tunes, were very numerous, and have...enjoyed an enduring popularity. [His sacred works are] remarkable not only for their quiet simplicity and natural melody, but [for] retaining a hold upon the religious world which is rarely achieved...

Lowell Mason has lived to see more fruit grown to maturity than falls to the lot of most workers in the fields of human education, and he dies, leaving an enduring monument behind him. He has taught the people their sacred songs, whoever else may have made their laws.
— *The Philadelphia Bulletin*, August 13, 1872[48]

Notes

[1]William A. Mowry, "Reminiscences of Lowell Mason." *Education* 13 (February 1893): 336-37.

[2]Bruce Dunbar Wilson, "A Documentary History of Music in the Public Schools of the City of Boston, 1830-1850." (Ph.D. diss., University of Michigan, 1973): vol. 1: 122.

[3]Ibid., 122-23.

[4]Letter to the author, August 20, 1986.

[5]Carol A. Pemberton, *Lowell Mason: His Life and Work.* (Ann Arbor, MI: UMI Research Press, 1985). Biographical information comes from this source unless otherwise indicated.

[6]Samuel F. Smith, "Recollections of Lowell Mason." *New England Magazine* 11 (January 1895): 649.

[7]Pemberton, 14. The trip is described in Lowell Mason's words; his letter to his family is quoted by his grandson, Daniel Gregory Mason in "How Lowell Mason Travelled to Savannah." *New England Magazine* 26 (April 1902): 238-40.

[8]Lowell Mason, *The Boston Handel and Haydn Society Collection of Church Music.* 9th ed. (Boston: Richardson, Lord & Holbrook, 1831), quoting the *Harmonicon,* London.

[9]Pemberton, 26.

[10]Ibid., 24. The letter was written in 1822.

[11]Ibid., 46.

[12]Mason's religious beliefs grew out of early training and a conversion experience in Savannah. His own statements attest to his faith and his commitment to the church. Pemberton, 13-16, 22, 99, 237 n.9.

[13]Pemberton, 55-56.

[14]Ibid., 62.

[15]*Dwight's Journal of Music* 12 (February 27, 1858): 380.

[16]Pemberton, 65.

[17]Ibid., 69.

[18]Ibid., 74.

[19]Robert W. John, "Origins of the First Music Educators Convention." *Journal of Research in Music Education* 13, no. 4 (Winter 1965): 209, 216-17.

[20]Pemberton, 91, from an eyewitness account by James C. Johnson left in an undated, handwritten document now in the Medfield, Massachusetts Historical Society Collection.

[21]Pemberton, 92.

[22]Wilson, vol. 2: 80-86.

[23]Ibid., 109-29.

[24]Ibid., 208-16.

[25]Ibid., 220-21. For more detailed information on events leading to August 28, 1838, and on the historic concert of

August 14, 1838, see Pemberton, "Critical Days for Music in American Schools," *Journal of Research in Music Education*, forthcoming 1988, and "Singing Merrily, Merrily, Merrily," *American Music*, forthcoming 1988.

[26]Pemberton, *Lowell Mason*, 117.

[27]Ibid., 131-33.

[28]Ibid., 53.

[29]Ibid., 181, from a letter to Yale Divinity School.

[30]Ibid., 167. A more detailed presentation of Mason's concepts is in his "Song in Worship: An Address." (B11)

[31]Pemberton, *Lowell Mason*, 166.

[32]Ibid., 191, in a letter to W. W. Killip dated February 26, 1860.

[33]George Brandon, letter to the author, March 6, 1987.

[34]William E. Studwell, "Lowell Mason: The Modest Music Maker," *The American Organist* 20, no. 7 (July 1986): 84-85 explores this practice and its ramifications for Mason's reputation as a hymn-tune writer.

[35]Henry Lowell Mason, *Hymn Tunes of Lowell Mason: A Bibliography* (Cambridge: The University Press, 1944) presents his conclusions. Contrast Ellen Jane Lorenz Porter, "A Hymn-Tune Detective Stalks Lowell Mason," *Journal of Church Music* 24 (November 1982): 7-11, 31-32.

[36]Pemberton, *Lowell Mason*, 172.

[37]*Historical Statistics of the United States Bureau of the Census* (Department of Commerce, 1975) and *Consumer Price Index* (Bureau of Labor Statistics, 1987) provided data upon which the computations were made.

[38]Lowell Mason, *Musical Letters from Abroad* (Boston: Oliver Ditson Co., 1853. Reprint. New York: Da Capo Press, 1967), 143-44.

[39]"The Germania Musical Society," *Dwight's Journal of Music* 5, no. 24 (September 16, 1854): 189.

[40]Pemberton, *Lowell Mason*, 155.

[41]*Dwight's Journal of Music* 3 (April 16, 1853): 15.

[42]*Dwight's Journal of Music* 39 (August 1879): 30.

[43]Pemberton, *Lowell Mason*, 206.

[44]"Lowell Mason," *Dwight's Journal of Music* 32, no. 11 (August 24, 1872): 296.

[45]Manuscript, "A Treatise on Harmony": 5-7. This document is part of the Special Collection at the MENC Historical Center, College Park, MD.

[46]Pemberton, *Lowell Mason*, 136.

[47]Ibid., 208.

[48]"Lowell Mason," *Dwight's Journal of Music*, 32, no. 11 (August 24, 1872): 296.

Catalog of Works

This catalog describes each of Lowell Mason's music publications, showing the individuality of each work and the diversity of the works overall. Because these works are now comparatively rare, many readers cannot readily examine the volumes themselves. Though admittedly a poor substitute for firsthand inspection, this catalog will give readers an indication of what they would see, were they able to look for themselves.

Preparation of such a catalog was originally inspired by the listing of works published in *Lowell Mason: "The Father of Singing Among the Children"* by Arthur L. Rich (Chapel Hill: The University of North Carolina Press, 1946). In his book, Dr. Rich indicated the availability of Mason publications in libraries "noted for the richness of their Lowell Mason collections," (138) offering data this writer has found to be reliable, allowing for slight changes in library holdings over time.

The material in the Rich book provided an excellent starting point. Then in October 1969, while preparing a doctoral dissertation, this writer surveyed 125 college, university, city, and private libraries with respect to their Mason holdings. These libraries, ranging from some of the nation's largest to some of the nation's most specialized small libraries, represented all parts of the United States. About ninety percent responded. The fact that Mason's publications are still found in libraries from coast to coast dramatizes his national impact: his books reached all corners of the nation in the 1800s, and many still survive.

The catalog below is limited to works Lowell Mason completed alone or with collaborators. Though his music was widely anthologized, instances of that practice are not reflected here. Mason sometimes contributed an "Elements" section to someone else's work, at times lifted verbatim from one of his own books. Such volumes are not listed, nor are those in which Mason is cited as an "inspiration" to the editor.

When the size of the volume, the number of pages, and/or the number of compositions is stated, *the numbers are approximate.* Exact reporting of such details would be cumbersome because these publications often ran through successive editions, sometimes with modifications in format and content. This writer is responsible for the annotations unless otherwise indicated.

Titles are spelled as printed. Generally, prefatory statements are paraphrased; exact words of Mason (or others) are in quotation marks. Prefatory passages of his works are often unsigned, but it is assumed that the writing was Mason's or that the statements had his approval. References to secondary sources are indicated through the use of codes assigned in the Bibliography below. Numbers that follow the code numbers are page references.

* * * * * * * * * *

1812

W1. "Ordination." composed and dedicated to the singing society in Dover [Massachusetts]. Words by Dr. Dodderidge. n.p., n.d.

> 25.5 X 35 cm. For voices and unspecified instruments. Both SAB and SATB sections with the first twenty lines of text given to alternate solo voices. At one point a short three-voice imitative passage ap-

pears. Introduces the Doxology near the end but closes with an "exultant climax, 'Finale Halleluia Chorus.'" (B184, 68)

This work is Mason's first composition, written for the ordination of Ralph Sanger in Dover, 1812. (B210, 5) Information about the performance and the young conductor is available in "Musical Reminiscences of an Octogenarian," identified only as L.L.A., in *The Record*, Boston, January 8, 1881. L.L.A, a Medfield teacher in 1810, adds that Lowell Mason left his local musical activities to his brother Johnson upon leaving Medfield for Savannah in 1812. (Source: MENC Historical Center Collection)

1822

W2. *The Boston Handel and Haydn Society Collection of Church Music; being a selection of the most approved psalm and hymn tunes; together with many beautiful extracts from the works of Haydn, Mozart, Beethoven, and other eminent modern composers.* Never before published in this country: The whole harmonized for three and four voices, with a figured base for the organ or pianoforte. Circulated for public worship or private devotion. Boston: Richardson & Lord, 1822, 1823, 1825, 1826, 1827, 1828, 1829; Boston: Lord & Holbrook, 1830, 1831, 1832; Buffalo: O.G. Steele, 1833; Boston: Carter, Hendee & Company, 1833, 1834, 1835; Boston: J.H. Wilkins & R.B. Carter, 1836, 1837, 1838, 1839. Reprint. New York: Da Capo Press, 1973, unabridged republication of the first edition, 1822, with a new introduction by H. Wiley Hitchcock.

> About 13 X 23 cm., 360 pages. Contains an Elements of Music section with vocal exercises, hymn and psalm tunes, choral sentences and anthems with and without solo passages, Anglican chants, and an index of tunes. A mixture of open and close score; figured bass with nearly all of the compositions. Most of the music is four-part with three- and five-part pieces interspersed.

> See B210, 31-39, on the goals of this tunebook, Mason's efforts to find a publisher, his association with the Handel and Haydn Society (including contract terms). Mason's name appeared on the title page

beginning with the ninth edition (1830). In that edition, Mason added about a hundred new tunes and altered others; he also replaced longer anthems with shorter, easier ones "more applicable...to public worship." (B210, 38)

1824

W3. "From Greenland's Icy Mountains." A missionary hymn by the late Bishop Heber of Calcutta. Composed and dedicated to Mary W. Howard, Savannah, Georgia. Boston: John Aston, n.d.; Boston: James L. Hewitt & Co., n.d.; Baltimore: Geo. Willig, Jr., 1824.

> Originally published as a soprano solo with keyboard accompaniment in F Major. Marrocco and Gleason's *Music in America* (B177) reprints the original version, Baltimore, 1824.

W4. *Select Chants, Doxologies &c. Adapted to the Use of the Protestant Episcopal Church in the United States of America.* Harmonized and arranged by Lowell Mason. Published according to Act of Congress. Boston: Richardson & Lord, 1824.

> 14.5 X 23.5 cm. 36 pages, Anglican chants. Single and double chants, some credited to various composers, including V. Novello and G.K. Jackson. SATB; figured bass. Stanza 1 under the top line, 2 under the second line, etc. with remaining stanzas under the fourth vocal line.

1828-30

W5. *Choral Harmony: Being a selection of the most approved anthems, choruses, and other pieces of Sacred Music; Suitable for Singing Societies, Concerts, and various Public Occasions.* The vocal parts in score: the instrumental accompaniment adapted to the organ. By the Boston Handel and Haydn Society. Edited by Lowell Mason, Member of the Same. Published in several sections beginning in 1828 by Richardson & Lord, Boston; collected and republished under a new copyright in 1830 by Richardson, Lord & Holbrook.

25 X 30 cm. 208 pages. Choruses, motets, recitatives, anthems, sentences, chorales, canons, hymns, duets, doxologies, quartettes. 54 compositions, mostly SATB, a few SATB plus solo, and some SSATB. Open score plus keyboard.

Most works include no composer identification; even Mason's "Missionary Hymn" is without identification. Exceptions: a motett by Dr. Crotch, and anthem by Broderip, an excerpt from a Mozart mass, the motett "Far, far o'er hill and dell" by Benjamin Carr, the anthem "When lost in wonder" by Dr. Callcott, and a hymn "When I can read my title clear" by Thomas Hastings.

1829

W6. *The Juvenile Psalmist; or, The Child's Introduction to Sacred Music.* Prepared at the request of the Boston Sabbath School Union. Boston: Richardson, Lord & Holbrook, 1829, 1830.

14 X 13 cm. 32 pages. Psalm and hymn tunes. Two and three part writing with top two voices on the top staff: SS or SB, TB; others SSB, SAB. No accompaniment. The "Advertisement" indicates that the top line is for sopranos, the middle line for boys or girls, and the bass line for men. Among the tunes are Old Hundred, Duke Street, and Missionary Hymn. The index shows a total of 28 tunes, a mixture of LM, CM, SM, and a few irregular meters.

Brief rudiments of music. Meant as an introduction to psalmody. Consists of twelve pages in six short lessons, using question-and-answer format. "The rudiments of music have been explained in a very plain and easy manner, and although brief, they are believed to be amply sufficient to enable children to read music, and sing understandably....One or two hours in the week devoted to this subject [singing] would soon render this exercise in Sabbath Schools pleasing and profitable, and would also prepare the way for a much more appropriate performance of Psalmody in public worship." (Advertisement)

On the flyleaf in his copy, Lowell Mason wrote, "This is the first book ever published for S. Schools in this country, &, as far as I know, in any other." (B184, 178) Lowell Mason was mistaken. Three American Sunday School books predate his: *The Sunday School Music Book* by E. Osborn (1826); *Juvenile Psalmody* by Thomas Hastings (1827); and *Sabbath School Psalmody* by Ezra Barrett (1828). For details on these books and further discussion of *The Juvenile Psalmist*, see B57, 218-40.

W7. "The Lord's Prayer." For Men's Voices. Boston: Oliver Ditson & Co., 1829. Reprint. Oliver Ditson Octavo Edition #1732.

One page. TTBB, chordal. No solo passages. Separate lines of text use variations of musical themes; no exact repetition of themes. Simple, unaccompanied setting.

1830

W8. "Watchman! Tell Us of the Night, a Missionary or Christmas hymn by Bowring." Sung at the monthly concert, Park Street Church, Boston. Music by Lowell Mason. Boston: C. Bradlee, 1830.

30 X 20 cm., 2 pages. For two solo voices, SAB chorus, keyboard accompaniment. Three stanzas plus a coda.

1831

W9. *Church Psalmody: a collection of psalms and hymns, adapted to public worship.* Selected from Dr. Watts and other authors. Boston: Perkins & Marvin, 1831, 1832, 1833, 1834, 1837, 1838, 1839; Boston: T.R. Marvin, 1842, 1843, 1844, 1846, 1848, 1849, 1852, 1854, 1855, 1856, 1857, 1858, 1859, 1862, 1864.

Co-editors: Lowell Mason and David Greene.

No music; texts only. See also *Manual of Christian Psalmody* (1832), W14, and *Union Hymns* (1834), W23.

W10. *The Juvenile Lyre; or Hymns and Songs, Religious, Moral, and Cheerful, Set to Appropriate Music, for the use of primary and common schools.* Boston: Richardson, Lord & Holbrook, 1831, 1832; Boston: Carter, Hendee & Company, 1833, 1835; Boston: J.H. Wilkins & R.B. Carter, 1836.

Co-editors: Lowell Mason and Elam Ives, Jr.

23 X 13.5 cm., 72 pages. Strophic songs with sacred or secular texts. SSA, SA, SAB, or SS with bass clef instrument or vocal accompaniment. Much rhythmic variety, use of dotted notes and small note values (e.g., sixteenth notes). One anthem with a recitative: "Suffer the Little Children to Come Unto Me" and a footnote saying it was first sung at the Park Street Church by the Juvenile Choir July 4, 1830. Preface cites S.F. Smith, Andover Theological Seminary, as translator and contributor of many "beautiful original" texts. (B136; B57, 241-53.)

1832

W11. *The Choir; or Union Collection of Church Music, consisting of a great variety of psalm and hymn tunes, anthems, &c. Original and selected, including many beautiful subjects from the works of Haydn, Mozart, Cherubini, Nauman, Marcello, Mehul, Himmel, Winter, Weber, Rossini, and other eminent composers, harmonized and arranged expressly for this work.* Boston: Carter, Hendee & Company, 1832, 1833, 1834, 1835; Boston: J.H. Wilkins & R.B. Carter, 1836, 1837, 1838, 1839.

14 X 24 cm. 360 pages. Hymn and Psalm settings, anthems, sentences. SATB. Open score. Some editions include some figured bass. No accompaniment except for optional passages in some of the anthems. Unless otherwise noted, the music is arranged from the top staff down for tenor, alto, soprano ("counter tenor or second treble"), "base."

Much new music procured from European sources; many pieces composed especially for this work. Some material furnished in manuscript form by German and English composers. Many tunes in triple meter which is "effective and universally popular."

W12. "Hymn for the Fatherless and Widow Society." Words by S.F. Smith, music by Lowell Mason. n.p., October, 1832.

16 X 25 cm. 8 pages. SATB, unaccompanied but with "Symphony" or interlude sections. Treble solo voices used in two duets within the work.

W13. *Lyra Sacra: consisting of anthems, motetts, sentences, chants &c. Original and selected: most of which are short, easy of performance and appropriate to the common and various occasions of public worship.* Boston: Richardson, Lord & Holbrook, 1832.

15 X 25.5 cm. 384 pages. Anglican chants, hymns, Psalm settings, anthems, sentences, canons, occasional pieces such as Christmas music. Among the six canons is Mason's first published example in this form: "My Soul Doth Magnify the Lord" (B184, 199). Mostly SATB. Some SSATB, SAB, SA plus bass. Some solo and duet parts, some figured bass.

The preface indicates that works of the "masters are, in the present state of music education...too difficult...for choirs to perform, or for audiences to comprehend." (iii) This book provides suitable materials for use in American churches, such as works by Charles Zeuner and George J. Webb.

W14. *Manual of Christian Psalmody, a collection of psalms and hymns, for public worship.* Boston: Perkins & Marvin, 1832, 1833, 1837, 1838, 1840.

Co-editors: Lowell Mason and David Greene, with additional hymns by Rufus Babcock, Jr., pastor of the First Baptist Church of Salem. (cf. *Union Hymns*, 1834, W23)

Substantially the same as *Church Psalmody* (1831), W9, except for the Baptist hymns added by Babcock. No music; texts only.

W15. *Spiritual Songs for Social Worship. Adapted to the use of families and private circles in seasons of revivals, to missionary meetings, to the monthly concert, and to other occasions of special interest.* Utica, N.Y.: Hastings & Tracy & W. Williams, 1832; Utica, N.Y.: G. Tracy, 1837; Boston: Carter, Hendee & Co., 1834, 1836, 1837, 1839.

Co-editors: Lowell Mason and Thomas Hastings

15 X 9.5 cm. 162 pages. Short hymn tunes. Several separate texts for each tune. Keyboard scoring. Some SAB, SB, SATB; a few unison songs. Index of first lines and index of titles by subjects.

Preface denounces the use of "too much tasteless material," or too much which is "merely insipid" or that which has "profane associations in the minds of the public." Exhorts the young convert, the "older" Christians, and all other believers to join in singing these "devotional songs." The work was offered to counter Joshua Leavitt's book of revival songs, *The Christian Lyre*, 1831. (B210, 56) Format is like Leavitt's book, with tunes on one side and text on the other, but with variations of that pattern.

1833

W16. *Sabbath School Songs: or Hymns and Music Suitable for Sabbath Schools.* Prepared for The Massachusetts Sabbath School Society, and revised by the Committee of Publication. Boston: Massachusetts Sabbath School Society, 1833, 1834, 1835, 1836, 1841.

14 X 12 cm. 48 pages. 36 songs, including 5 hymn tunes and 20 musical settings by Mason in 3 parts. Simple, generally lighter music of a "more melodious character than is usual in common psalm tunes." (cf. B57)

W17. *Sacred Melodies, composed and arranged as solos, duetts, trios, quartetts, &c., with an accompaniment for the pianoforte.* Boston: Carter, Hendee & Company, 1833.

>   Co-editors: Lowell Mason and G.J. Webb

>   30 X 25 cm. 91 pages. Contents specified in the title. Open scoring with separate keyboard staves, no figured bass. Keyboard accompaniment; use of a flute obligato in one selection.

>   Pages 8-12 provide a musical setting of a hymn beginning "Hark, 'tis the holy temple's bell," with a note reading, "This beautiful hymn for Sabbath morning, was written and presented for publication in the work by John Quincy Adams (1767-1848), late President of the United States of America." (B184, 199-A)

1834

W18. *The Boston Collection of Anthems, Choruses, &c., Consisting of selections from the works of the most distinguished composers, appropriate to the various circumstances of singing societies, concerts, and exhibitions of sacred music.* With a separate accompaniment for the organ. Published by the Boston Handel and Haydn Society. Boston: Carter, Hendee & Company, 1834.

>   25 X 30 cm. 56 pages. Anthems, sentences, choruses, with and without solo passages. SATB, SSATB, SATTB with keyboard accompaniment, no figured bass. All the compositions are original by Lowell Mason (B184, 199-B). No prefatory statements.

W19. *Lafayette Music: consisting of a dirge, requiem, and ode, as performed in Faneuil Hall, Boston, on the occasion of the delivery of a Eulogy on the character of Lafayette, by Edward Everett, September 6, 1834.* Poetry by Grenville Mellen and Isaac McLellan, Jr. Music by Lowell Mason and George J. Webb. Boston: n.p., 1834.

25 X 31 cm. Three compositions: 1) "Dirge–Dead March" by Handel. Vocal parts added by Mason. SATB, plus organ, pp. 1-4. 2) "Requiem," words by Mellen; music by Mason. SATB plus organ with an organ introduction and accompaniment. A bass recitative in the middle; organ and choir ending, pp. 4-11. 3) "Ode" words by McLellan; music by Webb, pp. 11-18.

W20. *Manual of the Boston Academy of Music, for Instruction in the Elements of Vocal Music, on the System of Pestalozzi.* By Lowell Mason, Professor in the Academy. Boston: Carter, Hendee, & Company, 1834. Boston: J.H. Wilkins & R.B. Carter, 1836, 1837, 1838, 1841, 1843, 1844, 1845. Boston: Wilkins, Carter & Co., 1847, 1849. Boston: Rice & Kendall, 1853. New York: Mason Brothers, 1861.

15 X 10 cm. 252 pages. "The book begins with general observations on the Pestalozzian system as Mason understood it, a [brief] statement about his sources of information, and a summary of the advantages of cultivating vocal music. He then discusses appropriate classroom equipment for music teaching, qualifications for teachers, and–at the heart of the book–methods of teaching individual elements of music, e.g., rhythm, tempo, melody, intervals, transposition, dynamics, and articulation. Dozens of music examples are included. Explicit instructions are provided for the teacher, along with material to demonstrate or write on the chalkboard and questions to ask the students." (B210, 83; See also B74 and B212.)

W21. *The Sacred Harp or Eclectic Harmony: a new collection of church music, consisting of a great variety of Psalm and hymn tunes, anthems, &c., original and selected; including many new and beautiful subjects from the works of the most eminent composers, arranged and harmonized expressly for this work.* Cincinnati: Truman & Smith, 1834, 1835, 1836, 1837; Boston: Shepley & Wright, 1838, 1840; Cincinnati: Truman & Spofford, 1850. Also published in a shape-note version by Truman & Smith, 1834.

Co-editors: Lowell Mason and Timothy B. Mason, Professor in the Eclectic Academy of Music, Cincinnati

16 X 26 cm. 232 pages. Hymn and Psalm settings, sentences, set pieces, chants, anthems. SATB, some SA with "base instrument." A great number of "very beautiful compositions have been taken, *by permission*, from the *Handel and Haydn Society Collection; The Choir; Lyra Sacra*, and other musical publications of the senior Editor." (Advertisement, iv)

In the "Publisher's Advertisement" to the shape-note version, the editors remark that the book is printed in "patent notes" contrary to their wishes, "in the belief that it will prove much more acceptable to a majority of singers in the West and South." N.D. Gould (B98) says that it was necessary to use shape notes to sell the book in certain regions. He states that during the first year, 75,000 copies of the book were sold, but that people learned to read "regular" notes so that within two years, 85,000 copies in the standard notation were sold.

See also the two-volume set *The Sacred Harp: or Beauties of Church Music* (1841), W52, which adapted much material from this publication. Henry Lowell Mason, in a handwritten note now at the MENC Historical Center, says that this book is a successor to *The Ohio Sacred Harp* by T.B. Mason, 1834, and that it uses some of the same material as that book.

W22. *Sentences, or Short Anthems, Hymn Tunes, and Chants, Appropriate to Various Occasions of Public Worship.* Boston: Carter, Hendee & Company, 1834.

16 X 25 cm. 52 pages. Anglican chants, Psalm settings, anthems with and without solo parts. Short sentences and occasional pieces (e.g., "Charity Sentences, Appropriate on the Occasion of a Collection for the Relief of the Poor, particularly for widows and orphans"). SATB, open score, no figured bass.

Eight of the sentences, settings of the Beatitudes, were composed for the Bowdoin Street Church choir and sung there during a series of lectures on these texts. Favorably received there, they were published here.

W23. *Union Hymns: adapted to social meetings and family worship.* Selected from *Church Psalmody*, with additional hymns.

Boston: Perkins, Marvin, & Co., 1834; Boston: J.E. Tilton & Co., 1858.

Co-editors: Lowell Mason, David Greene, Rufus Babcock, Jr.
(Greene, a Yale graduate, worked with the American Board of Commissions for Foreign Missions; Babcock, a Baptist clergyman, became president of Waterville College.)

8 X 12.5 cm. 296 pages. No music; texts only. Preface indicates that this work is an abridgment of *Church Psalmody* (1831), W9, and *Manual of Christian Psalmody* (1832), W14, "adapted for use in smaller assemblies of Christian worshippers." Compilers hope to encourage "a more elevated, ardent, and consistent devotion in those assemblies...." (iii)

1835

W24. *The Boston Academy's Collection of Church Music: consisting of the most popular Psalm and hymn tunes, anthems, sentences, chants, &c., old and new; together with many beautiful pieces, tunes and anthems, selected from the masses and other works of Haydn, Mozart, Beethoven, Pergolesi, Righini, Cherubini, Romberg, Winter, Weber, Nägeli, Kübler, and other distinguished composers, arranged and adapted to English works expressly for this work: including, also, original compositions by German, English and American authors.* Published under the direction of the Boston Academy of Music. Boston: Carter, Hendee & Co., 1835; Boston: J.H. Wilkins & R.B. Carter, 1836, 1837, 1838, 1840; Boston: Wilkins, Carter & Co., 1842, 1843, 1844, 1849; Boston: Rice & Kendall, 1853; New York: Mason Brothers, 1857, 1863.

16 X 26 cm. 360 pages. Selections indicated by the subtitle. Open score with a few keyboard accompaniments. Mostly SATB, some solo sections.

Preface classifies the musical selections and discusses them. Adds a tribute to Nägeli who "has done more than any other man in modern times to promote the cause of musical education and church music."

W25. *Select Pieces of Sacred Music.* Published by the Boston Academy of Music. Boston: Shepley & Wright, 1835.

> 25 X 30 cm. 8 pages. Three pieces, each with separate choral and keyboard staves. Accompaniments follow vocal parts closely in these selections.
>
> (1) "My Soul, Inspired with Sacred Love." Music "adapted to a Favorite Italian Melody, and Arranged as a Solo, Duet, Trio and Chorus, with an Accompaniment for the Organ or Piano Forte." Text from Ps. 103, part 3 in *Church Psalmody* (1831), W9. The same melody appears in *The Choir* (1832), W11, as "Safford."
>
> (2) "The Sabbath Bell." Music by Neukomm arranged as a Duet, Trio or Chorus, with an Accompaniment for the Organ or Piano Forte by Lowell Mason. Organ or piano introduction, then a duet, trio, chorus.
>
> (3) Anthem. "He Shall Come Down Like Rain upon the Mown Grass." Musical Subject from Portogallo, Adapted to English Words, from the 72D Psalm, and Arranged as a Duet, with an accompaniment for the organ, or Piano Forte, by Lowell Mason.

1835-36

W26. *The Musical Library.* Boston: Otis, Broaders & Co., July 1835 to June 1836.

> Co-editors: Lowell Mason and G.J. Webb
>
> A monthly magazine. Each issue "must contain sixteen super royal quarto pages of music and four pages of printed matter." Total of 192 pages. Vocal pieces, piano and organ music. Reprints of Boston Academy of Music annual reports; notices of musical events; articles on musical taste, music education, teaching methods, the history of the Boston Handel and Haydn Society, the proper execution of rests and other technical matters; analyses of compositions.

The first issue contains an "Address" stating that the periodical will furnish "a choice collection of music...vocal and instrumental, sacred and secular...[as] a desirable companion in the parlor, the social circle, and in private instruction." Pieces will be selected from the best composers, "ancient and modern," with some original compositions. Also the magazine will "give instructions as to the formation and conducting of choral societies, and choirs of singers...and the best mode of proceeding, both in respect to church music, and to concerts...." (July, 1835, 1)

Total of 63 vocal compositions, 11 organ, 25 piano pieces appeared in the 12 issues. For a listing of specific contents, issue by issue, see B278, 441-46; for discussion of this and other music journals of the period, see B77 and B142.

1836

W27. *The Boston Academy's Collection of Choruses; being a selection from the works of the most eminent composers, as Handel, Haydn, Mozart, Beethoven, and others; together with several new and beautiful pieces by German authors, adapted to English words expressly for this work.* The whole arranged with an accompaniment for the piano-forte or organ. Boston: J.H. Wilkins & R.B. Carter, 1836; Boston; J.H. Wilkins & R.B. Carter and G.W. Palmer & Company, 1839, 1844, 1845.

24 X 30 cm. 263 pages. Choruses; anthems; mass, oratorio, and cantata excerpts, some with solo or duet parts. Some preceded by recitative sections. All open score with separate keyboard staves. Some suggestions for organ registration. No figured bass.

Preface says that many "beautiful and effective" pieces adapted from German sources are included, pieces never before appearing with English texts.

W28. *Collection of Anthems and Hymns.* Boston, n.p., 1836 (?).

Contains three items: "O Lord, who has taught us," altered from T. Marsh; "Bright Source of Everlasting Love" by Lowell Mason;

"Wake the Song of Jubilee,—Columbia's Birth-day, again we behold," by Lowell Mason. 8, 7, 8 pages respectively. Bound with *Occasional Psalm and Hymn Tunes* (1836), W31, (copy owned by the Newberry Library, Chicago).

W29. "Columbia's Birth-day, Again We Behold." Ode for 4th July, 1836; written by H.F. Gould, music by Lowell Mason. Boston: Shepley & Wright, 1836.

16 X 25 cm. 8 pages. SATB with keyboard. Could be performed without accompaniment except for an interlude between stanzas 2 and 3. Form: A A' A A'' with coda-like ending. Chromaticism in the text portion about the gushing of patriots' blood which, when poured in the furrow, permitted the growth of "the liberty tree."

W30. "I Will Extol thee, My God, O King." Boston: Kidder & Wright, 1836.

16 X 26 cm. 8 pages. Text from Ps. 145. SATB unaccompanied. "Symphony" parts optional as interludes. Some duet passages. Many short sections, contrasting in rhythm, tempo, and mood.

One of Mason's best known anthems, this composition was included in *The Modern Psalmist* (1839), W44, and other books.

W31. *Occasional Psalm and Hymn Tunes, Selected and Original: designed as supplementary to the several collections of church music in common use.* Boston: Melvin Lord, 1836 (numbers 1-3 singly); Boston: J.H. Wilkins & R.B. Carter, 1837 (numbers 1-3 bound); Boston: J.H. Wilkins & R.B. Carter, 1838 (numbers 4, 5 singly).

15 X 25 cm. Serial publication; about 135 pages. Mostly SATB, open score, occasional keyboard accompaniments. Many texts from *Church Psalmody* (1831), W9. No prefaces. Contains Anglican chants, Psalm and hymn settings.

W32. *The Sabbath School Harp: Being a selection of tunes and hymns, adapted to the wants of Sabbath schools, families, and social meetings.* Prepared for the Massachusetts Sabbath School

Society, and revised by the committee of publication. Boston: Massachusetts Sabbath School Society, 1836, 1837, 1838, 1841.

14 X 12 cm. 96 pages. Hymn and Psalm tunes. No composers or authors named. SAB and SATB. Close score, no figured bass. Three or four part music. No compound rhythms; mostly quarter and half note rhythm with 3/2 also common. Strophic compositions without refrains. No accompaniment. The 144 hymn texts are provided with 35 tunes by Lowell Mason. (B184, 310-11) Most of the texts are taken from other books, such as *Church Psalmody* (1831), W9.

Mason may have wanted to make this book "as different as possible from the traditional tunebook whose music he was working diligently to outmode. The *Harp* is a different shape (upright rather than oblong) and differs in its literary and musical format. Musically, Mason presented his music in condensed (piano) score by putting more than one vocal part on a staff. Literarily, he provided all the stanzas to each hymn whereas tunebooks frequently included only the first one or two. The omission of the rudiments was another significant departure...." (B57, 264-65 and 263-70)

The editor says this book is preferable to others of its type because the hymns are short enough to avoid fatiguing the singers and are "divested of all childish expressions, which are always offensive, even to young children." The book contains both old and new tunes, the new ones in an "easy and familiar style" to be "easily learned, sung and remembered by children, and by those who have not had much opportunity for musical cultivation." (4)

W33. *Selections for the Choir of the Boston Academy of Music, Vol.I.* Boston: Shepley & Wright, 1836.

368 pages. Publisher is sometimes listed as "the academy." For information on the capabilities of the academy choirs and concert repertoire, see B210, 74-78.

Vol. I. The Newberry Library catalog card bears this notation: "This work is not published, but has been printed by the academy....Almost all the music has full instrumental accompaniments." This volume contains only the vocal score.

1837

W34. *The Juvenile Singing School*. Boston: J.H. Wilkins & R.B. Carter, 1837, 1838, 1839, 1840, 1842, 1843, 1844.

Co-editors: Lowell Mason and G.J. Webb

This is the first songbook adopted by an American public school, namely, Hawes Grammar School, Boston. It contains the first song sung at the first public demonstration of American public school music students, "Flowers, Wildwood Flowers," composed by Lowell Mason. (For discussion of the demonstration concert, see B215.)

14 X 12 cm. 128 pages, 78 songs. Close score, mostly three-part writing. Strophic songs with and without refrains, usually with three or four stanzas. Occasional piano parts, usually optional chords. Much editing of tempo and dynamics.

Preface states that the book is to "furnish songs...for juvenile classes and singing schools; or for common schools, and academies." Some of the tunes are well-known, others original. "The variety is very great," making songs for different ages and circumstances available. Some songs from German school songbooks.

W35. *The Odeon: a collection of secular melodies, arranged and harmonized for four voices, designed for adult singing schools, and for social music parties*. Boston: J.H. Wilkins & R.B. Carter, 1837, 1838, 1839, 1840, 1841, 1842, 1846.

Co-editors: Lowell Mason and G.J. Webb

16 X 25 cm. 304 pages. Glees, songs, including a harmonized Tallis chant, the French national anthem, and others. Four voiced; some solo passages.

Preface states that the pieces selected have "a decided popularity." Many were known earlier as songs or duets but have been "harmonized for the first time or altogether newly arranged" and a few were "composed expressly for this work."

1838

W36. *The Boston Glee Book; consisting of an extensive collection of glees, madrigals, and rounds; selected from the works of the most admired composers, together with many new pieces from the German, arranged expressly for this work.* Boston: J.H. Wilkins & R.B. Carter, 1838, 1839, 1847; Boston: J.H. Wilkins & R.B. Carter, & G.W. Palmer & Co., 1841; Boston; J.H. Wilkins & R.B.Carter & Jenks & Palmer, 1844, 1845, 1846; Boston: Oliver Ditson & Co., n.d. Reprint of the 1844 edition by Wilkins and Carter. New York: Da Capo Press, 1977.

> 19 X 25 cm. 264 pages. Glees, madrigals, rounds, songs. Heavy reliance on English composers (Wilbye, Morley, Bennett, Este, Callcott, Danby). Mostly SATB, some with soli passages. No accompaniment because "no true glee singer will need it." (Preface)

W37. *The Lyrist, consisting of a selection of new songs, duetts, and trios, from recent works of various authors.* Boston: J.H. Wilkins & R.B. Carter, 1838.

> Co-editors: Lowell Mason and G.J. Webb

> 35 X 27 cm. 148 pages. Catches, songs, nocturnes in 2 and 3 parts, some for duets, trios or chorus. Keyboard accompaniment throughout, separate from the vocal score. Editors state that few of these pieces have been previously published in America; many are from German sources. They add that the music is not difficult; the piano parts are "of easy execution."

W38. *Musical Exercises for Singing Schools, to be used in connexion with the "Manual of the Boston Academy of Music, for Instruction in the Elements of Vocal Music."* Boston: G.W. Palmer & Company, and J.H. Wilkins and R.B. Carter, 1838; Boston: Wilkins, Carter & Co.,n.d.; New York: Mason & Law, 1851 (revised) (See W87).

58 X 36 cm. A set of 66 charts, 2 pages each, with music examples to illustrate rhythm patterns, scales. Six songs at the end: "America, Sicily, Medfield (by Mather)" and three by Lowell Mason: "Missionary Hymn, Boylston, and Hebron." All the examples and songs are in large notes as solo lines. Each chart (or lesson) refers to a specific section in the *Manual of the Boston Academy of Music* (1834), W20.

1837-38 (?)

W39. *The Juvenile Songster, consisting of thirty-five cheerful and moral songs, set to appropriate music, and designed for children, schools, & private families.* First edition, n.p.,n.d.; London: J. Alfred Novello, 1846.

18 cm. 56 pages. One and two-part simple strophic songs, close scoring. A third part can be sung by using the keyboard bass line as written or an octave higher. Total of 33 tunes, seven of them original by Mason. The book was issued simultaneously in Boston and London in late 1837 or early 1838 (B184, 329).

1838-39

W40. *Lessons in Vocal Music, Selected from Various Authors, and Arranged for Singing Schools and Classes.* n.p., n.d. The date above is suggested by Rich, B228, 170.

16 X 26 cm. Exercises in C Major, treble, one and two voices, 4/4 (except for one example in 6/8). Organized in three sections: diatonic intervals for one voice; diatonic intervals for two voices; chromatic scales and intervals for one and two voices. Exercises move from simple to more complex, using intervals in combination for review after each one is learned separately.

1838-40

W41. *The Seraph; a monthly publication of Church Music, consisting of Psalm and hymn tunes, chants, anthems, &c.; original and selected.* Boston: G.W. Palmer & Co., Nos. 1-10, 1838-39; Boston: Jenks & Palmer Nos. 11-24, 1839-40.

A series of eight-page leaflets, issued in 24 consecutive months from August 1838 through July 1840. Total of 192 pages, 189 compositions, some anthems and hymn tunes by Lowell Mason. Also Anglican chants and Psalm settings. Sold by subscription at one dollar per year. Open scoring, SATB, with piano added rarely. Many texts from *Church Psalmody* (1831), W9.

A one-sentence "Preface" at the beginning of each issue says the work is designed as a substitute for *Occasional Psalm and Hymn Tunes* (1836), W31, and is similar to it. Subscribers are to get *The Seraph* through the mail to provide new music for choir use each month.

For comparison with other music magazines of the day, see B18, 78-79, B77, and B142; for a listing of contents by issue, see B278, 456-62.

1839

W42. *The Boston Anthem Book: being a selection of anthems, collects, motetts, and other set pieces*. Boston: J.H. Wilkins & R.B. Carter, & Jenks & Palmer, 1839, 1841, 1843, 1844. New York: Mason Brothers, 1859.

15 X 25 cm. 296 pages. Hymns, collects, anthems, mass and oratorio excerpts. Mostly SATB, some SSA, ATB. Some choral works with solo passages. Accompaniment is sometimes included, other times optional. With and without figured bass; sometimes with only a bass line given.

"Most pieces are already well known and have become decidedly popular, but...being scattered through various publications...[they have] been difficult to procure...for the accommodation of choirs. Several new pieces, or those which were not previously published in this country, are added..." (Advertisement).

W43. *Juvenile Music*. Originally published in the Sabbath School Visitor. No. I. Furnished by Lowell Mason. Revised by the committee of publication. Boston: Massachusetts Sabbath School Society, 1839.

> This work is sometimes listed as *Juvenile Music for Sabbath-Schools* or *Juvenile Music for Sunday Schools*. 15 cm. 36 pages. Mostly one and two-page songs, strophic with extra stanzas (the second and following ones) printed below the music. Few text sources indicated. Mostly three-voice writing, close score. (B57, 275-76)

W44. *The Modern Psalmist; a collection of church music, comprising the most popular psalm and hymn tunes and occasional pieces in general use; together with a great variety of new tunes, anthems, motetts, sentences, chants, &c., by distinguished European authors; many of which have been composed or arranged expressly for this work; including, also compositions by the editor, never before published.* The whole constituting a body of church music probably as extensive and complete as was ever issued. Boston: J.H. Wilkins & R.B. Carter, 1839, 1840, 1841.

> 15 X 25 cm. 352 pages. Vocal exercises, Anglican chants, sentences, anthems with and without solo parts, hymn and Psalm tunes, motets, fuguing tunes, occasional pieces, one Stabat Mater. "671 musical compositions; 282 by European authors named in the front of the book, the balance of pieces being by Lowell Mason." (B184, 347) Mostly SATB, some SSATTB or SAB. Some solo, duet, trio passages. Organ is specified in some of the anthems; no accompaniment is provided for the hymns. Most of the music is on two staves.
>
> The editor believes his previous publications have contributed to "the rising music knowledge and taste in the country" by drawing from European sources. He tries to give subordinate parts a pleasing character and keep them all in a reasonable range. The choir selections are "mostly easy, short and adapted to various occasions."

1840

W45. *Little Songs for Little Singers.* Published under the sanction of the Boston Academy of Music. Boston: Perkins & Marvin, 1840.

14 X 12 cm. 96 pages. Songs, rounds, part and solo songs, some for special occasions (patriotic or other). Total of 90 songs; one, two, three part. A bass line is given for the keyboard or other instrument or an adult voice.

In the 1840 edition: "In a few instances the words have been taken from 'My Little Hymn Book,' or other similar children's books; and a small number of the tunes will be recognized as popular...melodies; but much the greatest part of the book is new."

In the 1855 edition: "The new edition...was issued on the request of many who knew of its previous issue. The previous edition was little advertised, little known, though it was superior to all other books of its type. The previous edition soon was out of print."

W46. "Thanksgiving Anthem." Words selected from the 147th Psalm, verses 12-20. Boston: Jenks & Palmer, 1840.

16 X 26 cm. 8 pages. SATB without accompaniment, but with some optional "Symphony" interludes. Brief points of imitation; some modulation, some efforts at word painting. Sectional with alteration in style and mood from one section to another.

1841

W47. *The Boston School Song Book; published under the sanction of the Boston Academy of Music.* Original and selected. Boston: J.H. Wilkins & R.B. Carter, 1841, 1844; Boston: Wilkins, Carter, & Co., 1845.

14 X 12 cm. 128 pages. 68 songs (mostly unison), 31 rounds, 11 sentences, 12 lessons, and 11 pages of "Questions on the Elements of Music." Strophic songs and a few Psalm settings are also included. (B184, 350) Close score, no figured bass, no accompaniment.

The objective of the book is to present suitable songs for beginners to accompany their study of the elements of music. These songs can be learned by rote; they will provide exercise for the children's voices and a relief from the "severer study of the elements."

W48. *Carmina Sacra: or Boston Collection of Church Music; comprising the most popular Psalm and hymn tunes in general use, together with a great variety of new tunes, chants, sentences, motetts and anthems, principally by distinguished European composers: the whole constituting one of the most complete collections of music for choirs, congregations, singing schools and societies, extant.* Boston: J.H. Wilkins & R.B.Carter, 1841, 1842, 1843, 1844; Boston: Wilkins, Carter & Co., 1845, 1846, 1847, 1848, 1850; New York: Mason Brothers, 1855, 1856, 1859, 1860.

> 16 X 25 cm. 352 pages. About 375 hymn tunes and 126 anthems, motets, sentences. Elements section includes exercises. Mostly SATB with some solo parts. Mixture of open and close score, some figured bass.

> Editor states that choirs need new music for variety and interest. He has included many recent compositions received "from distinguished European composers, which he could hardly feel justified in withholding from the public." A new feature in the book is the inclusion of codas for many of the Psalm tunes: "It is hoped they may add interest to the performance of psalmody."

W49. *The Gentlemen's Glee Book: consisting of a selection of glees for men's voices, by the most admired German composers.* Boston: J.H. Wilkins & R.B. Carter, 1841, 1842, 1845.

> 18 X 25 cm. 112 pages. Open score, no accompaniment. Some use of solos plus chorus.

> Notation from the Yale Catalog: "Most of the words have been translated, or have been written expressly for the music, by Mr. J.F. Warner." The music is in its original form except for alterations (mostly rhythmic) required to accommodate English poetry.

W50. *The Harp: A Collection of Choice Sacred Music; derived from the compositions of about one hundred eminent German, Swiss, Italian, French, English, and other European musicians;*

also original tunes by German, English and American authors, many of them having been arranged or composed expressly for this work. Cincinnati: Moore, Wilstach & Baldwin, n.d.; Cincinnati: Truman & Smith, 1841; Cincinnati: Moore, Wilstach, Keys & Co., 1859; Cincinnati: Wilstach, Keys & Co., 1859.

Co-editors: Lowell Mason and Timothy B. Mason

16 X 25 cm. 352 pages (1859 edition). Metrical and alphabetical indices. SATB, with tenor on top line, open score, figured bass. No keyboard except in some anthems.

Compilers indicate sources: "old and new melodies by German, English, and American composers"; arrangements of Gregorian chants; many "beautiful subjects from the most eminent composers, as Haydn, Beethoven, Mozart, Rossini, Weber, Winter, Romberg, Cherubini, Pergolesi, Marcello, Himmel, Mehul, Naumann, Righini, and other celebrated masters, arranged and harmonized expressly for this work, and not to be found in any other collection."

W51. "Hymn Composed for the Monthly Concert of Prayer, January, 1842 by H.Y." Boston: Kidder & Wright, Printers, c. 1841.

25 X 31 cm., SATB, unaccompanied.

W52. *The Sacred Harp: or Beauties of Church Music, a new collection of psalm and hymn tunes, anthems, sentences and chants, derived from the compositions of about one hundred eminent German, Swiss, Italian, French, English, and other European musicians; also original tunes by German, English and American authors, many of them having been arranged or composed expressly for this work.* Volume I, 24th edition (a continuation of *The Sacred Harp or Eclectic Harmony*, 1834, W21), Boston: Shepley & Wright, 1841; Volume II: Cincinnati, 1840; Boston: Kidder & Wright, 1850.

Co-editors: Lowell Mason and Timothy B. Mason

Volume I was advertised as "a collection of Psalmody by Lowell Mason and T.B. Mason"; Volume II names only T.B. Mason, though he expresses his gratitude to his brother who "composed and arranged many new tunes expressly for this volume."

According to a notation on the Newberry Library catalog card, Volume 2 was "an entirely separate publication" compiled by T.B. Mason. The subtitle on Volume 2 reads "A new collection of Psalm and hymn tunes, anthems, motetts, sentences and chants, derived from the highest sources of the musical talent of Europe and America."

1842

W53. "Blessed Be the Lord God, the God of Israel." Anthem. Suitable for Thanksgiving, Dedication, Ordination, or Other Occasions of Public Worship. Boston: J.H. Wilkins & R.B. Carter, 1842.

18 X 27 cm. SATB with occasional passages SSATB, unaccompanied. Open score. Keyboard interlude. Metronome markings indicated; performance time of three minutes indicated. Text on Ps. 72: 18, 19.

W54. *Book of Chants: consisting mostly of selections from the sacred Scriptures, adapted to appropriate music, and arranged for chanting. Designed for congregational use in public or social worship.* Boston: Wilkins, Carter & Co., 1842, 1843, 1844, 1846, 1847, 1850; Boston: Rice and Kendall, 1854; New York: Mason Brothers, 1860, 1862, 1864.

19 cm. 180 pages. Anglican chants. No composers but some authors named. Total "234 selections; 170 accompanying chants (double as well as single), several pages entitled 'Remarks on Chanting.'" (B184, 196) SATB, close score, no accompaniment.

Preface states that chant, though beautifully simple, is of great value because it is "so dissimilar to secular music, so easy for a congregation to learn," and has "susceptibility of genuine expression." Children should learn it in Sunday Schools. This book provides simple chants for congregational use. Dr. Crotch and Kocher are cited to reinforce the belief that "very few" dissonant chords should be used. "Utility and not novelty has been constantly kept in view in the preparation of this work." (iv)

W55. *Chapel Hymns: a selection of hymns with appropriate tunes; adapted to vestry or other social religious meetings.* Boston: T.R. Marvin, 1842.

> About 10 X 15 cm. 80 pages. Vertical format of the modern hymnal. Close score, four voices, no figured bass. Text under the staves, line by line, with additional stanzas below the music or on the opposite page. Index by first lines. Total of 94 texts.

> This work may be another response to the popular book by Joshua Leavitt (see W15). "The great interest felt in the subject of religion at the present time, and the character of the frequent meetings, for religious exercises and efforts, seems to call for a style of singing somewhat different from common Psalmody. The hymns (selected from various authors) are of an evangelical and experimental kind, suited to a revived state of religious feeling; the tunes are written in a style so simple and easy, and the several parts kept within so limited a compass that they may be performed with but little effort by the people at large...."

W56. "I Was Glad When They Said Unto Me. Anthem for the re-opening of the Bowdoin Street Church, August 21, 1842." Boston: Kidder & Wright, 1842.

> 16 X 26 cm. 8 pages. Open score. SATB unaccompanied with SSA trio in the middle. Chant-like writing appears at the beginning and end. Text from Ps. 122.

W57. *Periodical Psalmody: consisting of original and selected church music.* (April 1842) Boston: Kidder & Wright, 1842.

> 17 X 25 cm. 8 pages. First issue of a "work...proposed to be issued in numbers of eight pages and sold separately." Contains 15 hymn tunes and 7 Anglican chants. All the hymns are strophic, usually with 3 or 4 stanzas. No credits to poets or composers.

W58. "Three Patriotic Songs, Suitable for the Public Celebration of American Independence, on the 4th of July." Boston: Tappan & Dennet, 1842.

> 16 X 26 cm. 4 pages. SATB unaccompanied. Close score. (1) "For Thee, my Native Land, for Thee." AAB form, 4 measures repeated, then 6 measures. Strophic; 4 stanzas. (2) "For Freedom, Honor and Native Land." 3 stanzas, AAB form with the B section a refrain of 12 measures; the "A" section is 4 measures long. (3) "God Bless Our Native Land." 14 measures total, 3 stanzas.

W59. *Vocal Exercises and Solfeggios, with an accompaniment for the pianoforte. Adapted to the wants of private pupils, or classes in vocal music. Selected from Italian, French, German composers and adapted to Treble and Tenor, or Alto and Bass voices.* Boston: Wilkins, Carter & Co., 1842, 1844, 1845; Boston: Oliver Ditson & Co., 1850.

> 25 X 32 cm. 56 pages. Vocal exercises in various rhythms and at various levels of difficulty; 106 selections. Some use scales, others intervals, arpeggiated figures, or a combination of these. Embellishments, staccato, legato, and accents included. No texts. Compositions range from four measures to two pages. For solo or unison singing.

> "Introductory Remarks" state that the exercises are to be sung to vowel sounds. Most are for all voices, though a few are too high or too low for some singers. The exercises have been tested and proved in classes of students and in private tutoring. They should be practiced in many keys.

W60. "With Joy We Hail the Sacred Day." Hymn. Text on Ps. 122. Boston: J.H. Wilkins & R.B. Carter, 1842.

1843

W61. *The American Sabbath School Singing Book: containing hymns, tunes, scriptural selections and chants, for Sabbath schools.* Philadelphia: Perkins & Purves, 1843.

12 X 14.5 cm. 112 pages. Many compositions strophic, few with refrains. Many popular hymn tunes included. Close score. Four-part writing with stanza 1 of the hymns and psalms between the two staves and remaining stanzas after the composition or all stanzas between the lines. Index lists 154 hymns, 66 tunes, and 8 chants.

Introductory remarks argue for simple singable music for Sabbath Schools and for chanting.

W62. *Hartley Wood's Anniversary Book of Vocal and Instrumental Music, Practical and Theoretical, for the Fourth of July, Temperance and Anti-Slavery Occasions.* Principally composed by Lowell Mason, I.B. Woodbury, and H.W. Day. Boston: The Musical Visitor Office, #8 Court Square, 1843.

About 11 X 18 cm. 40 pages. 32 selections, written in a single treble line or keyboard scoring. Various temperance texts provided for Mason's "Missionary Hymn"; an anti-slavery anthem by Mason, "Echo for the Slave"; some texts also provided for "Yankee Doodle" and "Auld Lang Syne." A rare instance in which Lowell Mason became involved in political/social issues of his era; also an interesting association with H.W. Day, who became Mason's antagonist at about the time of this publication. (B210, 89-90)

Preface is two sentences, chiefly expressing hope that the book will be "useful in promoting the cause of Freedom from Tyrany [*sic*], Alcohol and Slavery."

W63. *Musical Service of the Protestant Episcopal Church in the United States of America, for Morning and Evening Prayer.* Designed for the use, not only of the choir, but of the whole congregation. Boston: J.H. Wilkins & R.B. Carter, 1843.

14 X 22 cm. 32 pages. Anglican chants. The reader is referred to Mason's *Book of Chants* (1842), W54, for the principles of chanting. "That work having received the decided approbation of several distinguished Clergymen and Laymen of the Episcopal Church, the Editor has at their recommendation adapted the usual Psalms for Morning and Evening Prayer to the same style of Chanting. This style

is believed to be more simple, natural and easy, and better adapted to congregational performance than the usual mode. It is certainly much more favorable to an appropriate utterance of the words, and when properly performed unites the power of music to impassioned declamation. To those whose desire it is to make music the means and not the end, the servant and not the mistress in the public services of religion, this work is most respectfully commended."

W64. *Songs of Asaph; consisting of original psalm and hymn tunes, chants, and anthems.* Boston: A.B. Kidder, 1843.

25.5 X 16 cm. 64 pages. Anglican chants, Psalm and hymn settings, anthems and other choir compositions. In general two types of pieces: (1) "set pieces" or tunes adapted to certain words; (2) tunes meant for various texts. SATB, close score, unaccompanied.

Mason had intended a series of publications to be issued one by one until enough material had accumulated for a full volume so that he could correct errors and "test out" tunes before the full volume was issued. Here 81 original pieces of sacred music were included, nine of them arrangements. (B184, 382)

W65. *Twenty-One Madrigals, Glees, and Part Songs: designed for choir practice, or chorus singing.* Selected mostly from old and distinguished composers. Boston: J.H. Wilkins & R.B. Carter, 1843, 1844, 1845, 1850.

Co-editors: Lowell Mason and G.J. Webb

25 cm. 72 pages. Open score, no accompaniment. Much editing. A mixture of SATB, SSATB, SATTB, and SSB. Table of contents identifies composers and types of selection. Works of Weekes, Ford, Bennet, Purcell, Cooke, Marenzio, Reichardt, Donato, Paxton.

1844

W66. "Gloria in Excelsis." As sung by the choir of the Central Church, Boston. Composed, and most respectfully dedicated to the Rev. Wm. M. Rogers, by Lowell Mason. Boston: A.J. Wright, 1844.

> 25 cm. 4 pages. SATB, unaccompanied. Full choir alternates with solo portions. Opens with an "allegro maestoso" (SATB); includes a chant-like section.

W67. "Songs, for the Boston City Celebration of American Independence, July 4th, 1844." Boston: A.J. Wright's Steam Power Press, 1844.

> About 15 X 25 cm. One page (Library of Congress copy, perhaps incomplete). Two selections: (1) "My Native Land," five stanzas of text, arranged with a musical opening phrase for solo soprano or sopranos joined in subsequent phrases by SAB voices; (2) Anglican chant of seven measures duration, ten stanzas of text.

W68. "Songs of Chenaniah, No. 1." Consisting of original church music by Lowell Mason. Boston: 1844.

> 16 X 26 cm. 8 pages, 4 entries. Settings of hymns, mostly SATB, but some SSAA. No accompaniment; close score. No prefatory remarks. The work is named for Chenaniah, a chief of the Levites skilled in music. See I Chronicles 15: 22, 27. (B184, 385-386)

W69. *The Vocalist; consisting of short and easy glees, or songs, in parts.* Arranged for soprano, alto, tenor, and bass voices. Boston: Wilkins, Carter & Co., 1844, 1845, 1847, 1848, 1849, 1850.

> Co-editors: Lowell Mason and G.J. Webb

> 19 X 25 cm. 200 pages. Choral scoring, no accompaniment. Works by Nägeli, Danzi, Gartner, Weigl, Immler, Beghardi, Kreutzer, Silcher, Mendelssohn, Tobler, F. Schmidt, Berner, Zumsteeg, Himmel, Naumann, Gersbach, Mohling, Karow, and others ("chiefly German sources," according to the "Notice"). Words are either a free translation or an imitation of the original texts.

1845

W70. *The Psaltery, a new collection of church music, consisting of psalm and hymn tunes, chants, and anthems; being one of the most complete music books for church choirs, congregations, singing schools, and societies, ever published.* Published under the sanction, and with the approbation of the Boston Academy of Music, and the Boston Handel and Haydn Society. Boston: Wilkins, Carter & Company, 1845, 1846, 1847, 1848, 1851; New York: Mason Brothers, 1858, 1860.

Co-editors: Lowell Mason and G.J. Webb

15 X 24 cm. 352 pages. About 450 hymn and Psalm tunes, 15 anthems, 75 chants. No accompaniments; a few interludes. Figured bass.

A prefatory section notes musical characteristics. The rhythmic variety is greater than in previous works. The harmony will be "more natural, easy, dignified, and church-like" than before, models being the old Italian and English masters (e.g., Palestrina, Purcell, and Tallis) "unrivalled for the simplicity and sublimity of their church harmonies, and the highest ambition of the editors has been to follow the example of these illustrious composers." Variety has been increased by the use of II, III, and VI chords. "A number of the tunes have been harmonized [so] as to admit...the transposition of the treble and the tenor." Minor scales have been used. "There are few hymns which could not be sung in minor, for what counts is reverence, solemnity, and humility."

W71. "Songs Prepared for the City Celebration of 4th July, 1845." Boston: A.B. Kidder, 1845.

17 X 19 cm. 4 pages. Three short strophic songs for mixed chorus. The context in which these songs was used is described in B210, 129-31, under the headings "The Final Years in Boston: Community Leadership in Music."

1846

W72. *The Boston Chorus Book; consisting of a selection of the most popular choruses, from the works of Handel, Haydn, and other eminent composers, arranged in full vocal score, with an accompaniment for the piano forte or organ.* Boston: Wilkins, Carter & Company, 1846, 1850; New York: Mason Brothers, n.d.

> 28 X 37.5 cm. 65 pages. Total of nine selections: four by Handel, two by Righini, one each by Rossini, Mozart, Haydn. Choruses, mass and oratorio excerpts. Mostly SATB, some with duets. Keyboard accompaniment. Open scoring plus a separate keyboard part. Markings for dynamics and tempo. Texts in English.

> These pieces were first printed for the use of teachers' meetings at the Boston Academy of Music.

W73. *The Cherokee Singing Book.* Prepared for the American Board of Commissioners for Foreign Missions. Boston: Alonzo P. Kenrick, 1846.

> Co-editors: Lowell Mason and George Guess

> Guess "came to fame as the inventor of the ingenious Cherokee syllabary whereby thousands of illiterate Cherokee were enabled within a reasonably limited time to read and write in their own language." (B184, 422)

> Begins with an "Elements" section in Cherokee, including music examples and exercises. Main body of the book contains about 120 psalm and hymn tunes with Cherokee texts, but titles, tempo markings, and composers' names are in English. Lowell Mason's tunes and arrangements include Hamburgh [*sic*], Olmutz, Lathrop, Olivet, Missionary Hymn, Antioch ("arranged from Handel"), and many others. Additional composers/compilers named include Arne, Purcell, Tansur, Tucker, Pleyel, Arlington, Ravenscroft, Haydn, Mozart, Giardini, Rousseau, von Weber, Hastings, Hatton, Dutton, Oliver, and Mrs. Cuthbert.

Psalm and hymn tunes are generally in four-voiced, TASB arrangement in open score, with neither accompaniment nor figured bass. A
few simple, unaccompanied anthems are included: "Come, Ye Dis-
consolate" by Webbe with solo and "Trio or Semi-Chorus" sections
and "Away with Melancholy," unattributed, for soprano/alto voices.
Indices of tunes are provided in Cherokee and in English.

W74. *The Primary School Song Book.* In two parts. The first
part consisting of songs suitable for primary or juvenile singing-
schools; and the second part consisting of an explanation of the
inductive or Pestalozzian method of teaching music in such
schools. Boston: Wilkins, Carter, & Co., 1846, 1847, 1849.

Co-editors: Lowell Mason and G.J. Webb

9.5 X 15.5 cm. 96 pages. Unison, two, and three-part songs, rounds,
with several texts for some tunes. Close score with two treble vocal
lines on the upper staff. No accompaniment but in a few instances, an
optional part for keyboard or a bass instrument.

Preface advocates that children be taught first by rote. This books
furnishes mothers and teachers with material for rote learning as well
as for reading. Many of the songs come from German sources because "Germans excel in children's songs." Some of these selections
were introduced in the United States by Woodbridge and published
earlier in *The Juvenile Lyre* (1831), W10. Other selections are new.
Among sources names are Nägeli, A. Weber, Reichardt, Harder.

1847

W75. *The Choralist: a collection of sacred music, consisting of
psalm and hymn tunes, chants and anthems.* Boston: 1847.

16 X 26 cm. A serial publication, 8 pages per issue. Four issues appeared. Hymn tunes, SATB. Open score, no accompaniment. Some
of the tunes are presented in two versions: one with the melody in the
top line of the four parts, the other with the melody printed immediately above the bass line. "Six titles [of hymn tunes included in

the 32 pages published] are listed by Henry Lowell Mason as original hymn tunes by Lowell Mason." (Yale Catalog)

W76. *The Song-Book of the School-Room; consisting of a great variety of songs, hymns, and scriptural selections with appropriate music, arranged to be sung in one, two, or three parts; containing, also, The Elementary Principles of Vocal Music, prepared with reference to the inductive, or Pestalozzian method of teaching: designed as a complete music manual for common, or grammar schools.* Boston: Wilkins, Carter & Co., 1847, 1848, 1850, 1851; New York: Mason Brothers, 1856, 1858, 1860.

Co-editors: Lowell Mason and G.J. Webb

11 X 18 cm. 224 pages. Short strophic songs, about one page each, most in three parts. Close score, no accompaniment. Vocal exercises included. Some special occasion songs, such as "Songs for the 4th of July." A full "Elements" section, including study questions, appears at the end of the book (unlike the usual arrangement with that section at the front).

Attention is called to the inductive method of the "Elements" section. "The editors...present this little volume to parents, teachers and pupils believing it not only free from that which is low, inelegant and pernicious, but that the songs, while they are cheerful and pleasing, will be found to accord with the efforts of those who labor to make our children better and happier."

W77. "Songs, for the Boston City Celebration of American Independence, July Fourth, 1847." Copyright deposited June 4, 1847. It is not known whether the work was actually published, and if so, by whom and when.

1848

W78. *The Congregational Tune-Book: being a collection of popular and approved tunes, (mostly from The National Psalmist) suitable for congregational use.* Boston: Tappan, Whittemore, & Mason, 1848; New York: Mason Brothers, 1854.

Co-editors: Lowell Mason and G.J. Webb

17 X 13.5 cm. 96 pages. Open score. Psalm and hymn tunes, strophic. Some sources of the tunes indicated. SATB. Of the 87 tunes, 65 are in L.M., C.M., or S.M.

The book was "issued in compliance with numerous requests from different sections of the country...to supply the wants...[where] Congregational Singing has been introduced." *The National Psalmist* (1848), W79, is more clearly intended for choirs, this book for congregations. The harmonization and arrangements are the same in both books. Tunes in this volume are truly "congregational in their character and style." The reader is referred to *The National Psalmist* for more discussion of congregational and choir singing.

W79. *The National Psalmist; a collection of the most popular and useful psalm and hymn tunes; together with a great variety of new tunes, anthems, sentences, and chants; the whole forming a most complete manual of church music for choirs, congregations, singing-schools, and musical associations.* Boston: Tappan, Whittemore, & Mason, 1848, 1849.

Co-editors: Lowell Mason and G.J. Webb

16 X 24.5 cm. 352 pages. Contents as indicated, plus some oratorio excerpts. Mostly SATB, some SSATB, SATTB. Mixture of open and close score. Figured bass used. Descriptive tables indicate difficulty levels. Tunes categorized according to metric patterns. Music given without accompaniment.

The editors summarize the role of Psalmody in Christian history, the reform movement in American churches, and subsequent improvements in church music. They call for congregational tunes to accommodate the singing of all and point out the necessity of congregational and choir music, separate but interrelated. Practical matters, such as tempo for singing, ways of introducing new tunes, and similar matters, are covered.

1849

W80. *Fifty-Nine Select Psalm and Hymn Tunes, for public or private worship.* Issued by the publishers of *Carmina Sacra, or Boston Collection* [1841, W48], for gratuitous distribution to all who may purchase that work, copy for copy. Boston: Wilkins, Carter & Co., 1849.

> 16 X 25 cm. 35 pages. Contents as stated. Choral scoring. Figured bass throughout. SATB and SSB.

> The publishers state that "the selection and preparation of the tunes has been made entirely without the aid of the editors of the *Carmina Sacra* [W48], who are consequently in no way responsible for the production." Yet the book was distributed with that earlier work. No individuals are named in connection with the preparation of this volume.

W81. *The Hymnist: a collection of sacred music, original and selected.* Nos. 1, 2. Boston: Tappan, Whittemore & Mason, 1849.

> Eight-page serial, co-edited by Lowell Mason and William Mason.

1850

W82. *Cantica Laudis, or The American Book of Church Music: being chiefly a selection of chaste and elegant melodies, from the most classic authors, ancient and modern, with harmony parts; together with chants, anthems, and other set pieces; for choirs and singing schools: to which are added tunes for congregational singing.* New York: Mason & Law, 1850. Boston: Tappan, Whittemore and Mason, c. 1850.

> Co-editors: Lowell Mason and G.J. Webb

> About 15 X 25 cm. 384 pages. Anglican chants, hymn and Psalm tunes, anthems, mass and oratorio excerpts. Vocal exercises in the

"Elements" section. About 450 hymns and chants plus 65 choir selections. SATB, mostly open score. Figured bass and "symphonies" or interludes provided in some of the choir music. No other accompaniments.

Contains a two-page preface plus an introduction to "Congregational Tunes." The preface defends the practice of arranging works from the masters. The editors contend that many lovely themes are useful, though their original forms might be impractical and unsuitable for church use. They note that the words "arranged from" can mean little or much arranging. "The greater part of the tunes without any name affixed [identifying composers] are taken from classic writers, or have been suggested by passages from them, and have only been composed by the editors." In italics, this additional note is included: "Therefore, they are found nowhere else and hereby are claimed as property." The choir music is divided into two parts: "people's tunes" which are easy to perform and understand (often popular German tunes); "classic tunes" which are more difficult to execute and understand.

Congregational tunes are divided into two classes:

I. Tunes fit for use according to these standards: placements within the usual vocal ranges; ease of melody; use of the oldest, easiest, and "most natural" rhythms. The easiest tunes are marked "1" in the book; those marked "2" are also fairly easy, though not as easy as "1."

II. Tunes too difficult for the ordinary congregation (by the editors' standards, with unequal note lengths being one measure of difficulty) are marked "3." "The true congregational style is a strictly syllabic union of words with tones and admits only of notes of two lengths, long and short." (295)

W83. *The Choral Advocate and Singing-Class Journal.* New York, June 1850-June 1853. Darius E. Jones, Editor; Lowell Mason and G.J. Webb, Boston corresponding editors.

Monthly 16-page octavo magazine. The last four pages of each issue contained musical compositions. The journal sought to be of use to choir members, choristers, and singing classes. Mason published many articles and musical items in this journal, 1850-1853. (See B8 for examples; B228, 448-49, for discussion.)

W84. *The Hymnist.* Boston: n.p., 1850.

16 X 26 cm. 203 pages. Unaccompanied hymn settings. Some figured bass.

W85. *The New Carmina Sacra: or Boston Collection of Church Music. Comprising the most popular psalm and hymn tunes in general use, together with a great variety of new tunes, chants, sentences, motetts, and anthems; principally by distinguished European composers: the whole being one of the most complete collections of music for choirs, congregations, singing schools and societies, extant.* Boston: Wilkins, Carter & Co., 1850, 1851; Boston: Wilkins, Rice & Kendall, 1852; Boston: Rice & Kendall, 1853; Boston: Rice, 1854; New York: Mason Brothers, 1855, 1856, 1857, 1858, 1859, 1860, 1861, 1862.

16 X 25 cm. 384 pages. Mostly SATB, some SATTB. Few include accompaniment, though an optional instrumental bass or keyboard part is sometimes added.

The preface to *Carmina Sacra* (1841), W48, is reprinted with a "Publisher's Notice" saying that the most popular and useful tunes of *Carmina Sacra* have been retained and the less useful ones dropped. New tunes were added, some of them from Zeuner's *American Harp* (1832). This new volume, larger because of additions, is essentially a new work and will not replace *Carmina Sacra.*

1851

W86. *The Glee Hive: a collection of glees and part songs, selected and arranged for the use of the musical conventions, teacher's institutes, and classes of the Boston Academy of Music.* New York: Mason & Law, 1851; Revised and enlarged edition, New York: Mason Brothers, 1853.

Co-editors: Lowell Mason and G.J. Webb

Note: On August 15, 1851, a copyright deposit was made on this work, naming Lowell Mason and William Mason as co-editors. Mason & Law, New York, and J.P. Jewett & Co., Boston, were named as publishers. Why a different co-editor was named on the published work is not known; why the Boston publisher was dropped is not known.

18 X 26 cm. 88 pages. SATB and SSATB. Mixture of open and close scoring. Some piano accompaniments and introductions.

The 1853 edition was 112 pages, 17 X 25 cm. SATB unaccompanied works. The original edition was so popular that the enlarged edition "with 16 pieces added" was called for. (B184, 451)

Compositions by Auber, Marschner, Beethoven, Mendelssohn, Macfarren, Richter, Taylor, William Mason, Horsley, Zollner.

W87. *Large Musical Exercises.* Boston: Wilkins, Carter & Co., 1851; New York: Mason & Law, 1851.

See *Musical Exercises for Singing Schools* (1838), W38, and *Mason's Mammoth Musical Exercises* (1856), W98.

1852

W88. *Congregational Church Music: A Tune Book in Two Parts each separate. Part I. General Psalmody containing 163 Psalm Tunes arranged by Messrs. Goss, Turle, Hopkins, Horsley, Novello, Dibdin, and Lowell Mason. Part II. Anthems, Hymns and Chants; containing 46 compositions arranged for congregational use, forming a supplement to any tune book.* Evidently published in London, about 1852-1853.

Advertised in *Practice Songs for Classes: Chiefly selected from the Class-Books of Dr. Lowell Mason and designed to provide, for psalmody, and other classes, music suited for practicing articulate and expressive singing* (London: Ward & Co., a serial publication). Each issue contains musical selections for music classes. First issue is eight pages long; at least ten issues were published. The exact extent of Lowell Mason's contributions cannot be ascertained.

W89. *Mason's Hand-book of Psalmody: a collection of ancient and modern psalm and hymn tunes, chants and short anthems, for public worship and family use; arranged for four voices, with an organ or pianoforte accompaniment.* London: Houlston & Stoneman; Z.T.Purday, n.d.; New York: Mason & Law, n.d.

> 15 X 18 cm. 33 pages, paperback. Four parts, written in close score with alto and tenor written in smaller notes. On separate staves above, the alto and tenor are written again; text is placed by the vocal score. No preface.

> On the second page, Mason wrote, "This sheet is only a portion of a work intended to comprise from 100 to 120 pages of music, in accordance with the title-page, the whole of which will be completed and published very shortly." The projected work was never completed. Arthur L. Rich believes these few pages were completed in England in 1852 or 1853. (B228, 161, n. 39)

1854

W90. *The Hallelujah: a book for the service of song in the house of the Lord; containing tunes, chants, and anthems, both for the choir and the congregation; to which is prefixed The Singing School: a manual for classes in vocal music, with exercises, rounds, and part songs, for choir practice; also Musical Notation in a Nutshell: a brief course for singing schools; intended for skillful teachers and apt pupils.* New York: Mason Brothers, 1854; Boston: B.B. Mussey and Co., c. 1854; Boston: Sanborn, Carter & Bazin, 1856; Boston: Oliver Ditson & Co., 1882.

> 17 X 25 cm. 368 pages. Mostly SATB, some solo, duet, trio passages in choir selections. Open and close score. Figured bass. Contents as specified, plus Psalm and hymn tunes, carols, "motetts," sentences, fughettas, and "occasional pieces."

Choir and congregational tunes separated on the basis of difficulty. Editor states the proper tempo for congregational singing is "as fast as the words may be uttered consistently with dignity and solemnity or nearly as fast as they would be appropriately read." (B210, 167-68, discusses the work further.)

On May 25, 1854, a copyright deposit was filed for a work called *Specimen Tunes from the Hallelujah, a Collection of Church Music*. The title page (on file at the Library of Congress) indicates that the work was to be published separately on September 1, 1854, by Mason Brothers, 23 Park Row, New York. Either that work was never published, or all the copies have disappeared without a trace.

W91. *Musical Notation in a Nutshell. Intended for Skillful Teachers and Apt Pupils.*

See publication information under *The Hallelujah* (1854), W90, with which it was published.

W92. *School Songs and Hymns: selected for the Massachusetts Teachers' Institutes.* New York: Mason Brothers, 1854.

About 22 X 14 cm. 15 pages. Paper cover. Mix of sacred and secular music, with Psalmody and chants; secular music with texts about nature and patriotism.

Didactic texts, such as this text set to the tune "Dundee":

> How shall the young secure their hearts,
> And guard their lives from sin?
> Thy word the choicest rules imparts,
> To keep the conscience clean.

The music is written on three staves with the tenor on top, the first and second treble in the middle (melody in the upper treble line), and "base" line beneath.

W93. *The Singing School, or The Elements of Musical Notation, Illustrated with Numerous Exercises, Rounds, Part-Songs, etc.* New York: Mason Brothers, 1854.

An independent work, but published with *The Hallelujah* (1854), W90, and *The Young Men's Singing Book* (1855), W97. See publication information under those titles.

"Forty years' constant experience in teaching is enough to enable one to learn that he really knows but little; we dare not therefore assert that these definitions are always expressed in the most clear and intelligible language, or that they are always complete, or free from error." (W90, 6, about the "Elements")

1855

W94. *Guide to Musical Notation.* New York: Mason Brothers, 1855, 1856, 1857, 1858, 1859, 1860, 1861, 1862.

This was an independent work, but it was published as part of *The New Carmina Sacra* (1850), W85, after 1855.

Consists of 19 short chapters, 21 pages in *The New Carmina Sacra.* Brief explanations and abundant examples. The exercises are practical. For instance, after teaching the scale and basic rhythm patterns, Mason presents the same notes in various rhythm patterns with various texts: he moves directly from the scale into songs, getting students into actual singing quickly. Dynamic markings are used almost from the start. Paragraphs are numbered for quick, easy referencing.

W95. *The New Odeon: a collection of secular melodies, arranged and harmonized in four voices.* New York, Mason Brothers, 1855, 1862.

Co-editors: Lowell Mason and G.J. Webb

W96. *Sacred Songs for Family and Social Worship.* New York: American Tract Society, 1855.

Co-editors: Thomas Hastings and Lowell Mason

Hastings credits Mason for his "valuable counsel and aid, besides the generous contribution of 35 tunes of which he holds the copyright."

W97. *The Young Men's Singing Book: a collection of music for male voices. Intended for use in colleges, theological seminaries, and the social circle.* New York, Mason Brothers, 1855.

Co-editors: Lowell Mason and G.F. Root

17 X 24 cm. 256 pages. Glees, part songs, choir and congregational tunes, anthems, chants, pieces for patriotic and other special occasions, TTBB. Part IV (tunes for congregational use) SATB. No accompaniment. Open score except for the hymn and Psalm tunes.

The editors deplore the use of SATB material for male choirs. This book fills a long-felt need for music for men's voices. In congregational tunes all singers should sing the melody (this line is printed in larger notes than the other parts); an instrument can fill in the harmony. *The Hallelujah* (1854), W90, is acknowledged as the source for many of the tunes and "other pieces."

1856

W98. *Mammoth Musical Exercises: or, Musical Diagrams for the Singing Class.* Designed to save teachers much labor at the Black Board. New York: Mason Brothers, 1857. (Copyright filed in November 1856)

25 X 40" with 60 musical diagrams containing 132 practical exercises. Printed from type big enough to be seen across a schoolroom. Arranged progressively. Advertised in *The New York Musical Review and Gazette* (December 1856 and other issues) as a labor-saving device for teachers who must otherwise write out all these exercises on chalkboards in each room they use.

This publication was a new, enlarged version of *Musical Exercises for Singing Schools* (1838), W38, and *Large Musical Exercises* (1851), W87.

W99. *Mason's Normal Singer: a collection of vocal music for singing classes, schools, and social circles.* Arranged in four parts. To which are prefixed *The Elements of Vocal Music, with Practical Exercises.* New York: Mason Brothers, 1856.

> 13 X 19 cm. 192 pages. Chants, Psalm and hymn tunes, secular songs. Vocal exercises and practice pieces in the Elements section. SATB with optional keyboard accompaniment in some pieces. Close score. Total of 18 hymn and chant tunes for about 50 texts.

> "Normal" in the title means "right" or "correct." The main purpose of the music is to "awaken, quicken, draw out, and invigorate the 'emotive powers.'" It is also a source of pleasure and rest. Teachers should call attention to the moral implied in each song; the best possible poetry and music were used here.

> The "Elements" section is essentially the same as Mason's "A Complete Course in Elementary Instruction, Vocal Exercises and Solfeggios" included in Root's *The Academy Vocalist,* 1852. (B228, 162, 164)

1858

W100. "Just As I Am." New York: Mason Brothers, 1858.

> 19 X 29 cm. Hymn setting, close score. Text also used with a Bradbury hymn tune. Six stanzas. Musically unusual among Mason's hymn tunes in that it is set in g minor, 3/2 meter.

1859

W101. *The Sabbath Hymn and Tune Book, for the Service of Song in the House of the Lord.* New York: Mason Brothers, 1859, 1860, 1863, 1864, 1865; Hartford: Hamersly & Co., 1873.

> Co-editors: Lowell Mason, Edwards A. Park, and Austin Phelps

23.5 cm. vertically. Modern hymnal format. 510 pages. Chants, hymns, Psalm tunes, about 22 simple, hymn-like anthems. SATB, close score, no accompaniment. Three or four texts per tune, each text having several stanzas; about 1290 hymn texts. Extra texts printed beneath the tunes.

This book "departs from custom in several ways....[It] has a more detailed preface than any previous work by Mason....The book also contains more thorough indexing than Mason's previous works. These indices list tunes alphabetically and metrically, texts according to first lines, and compositions according to types (chants, anthems, doxologies...). The book offers three or four texts for each tune with alternate texts usually on the bottom half of the page and the tunes on the top. Moreover, Mason uses keyboard scoring with the melody in the soprano line as in modern practice, but alto and tenor parts are printed in smaller notes than the outer voices. The four parts are complete and free of the antiquated figured bass found in earlier books, yet singers are visually encouraged to follow the melody line (soprano) or the bass line." (B210, 168-69)

The material was published in four versions, including one for Baptist use, "identical to the original edition except for the addition of thirty-one Baptist texts set to eleven hymn tunes." (B210, 170)

1860

W102. *Music and Its Notation.* Boston: Oliver Ditson & Co., 1875.

This work seems to be a revision of *The Singing School or The Elements of Musical Notation* (1854), W93. It appeared in Root's *The Diapason* (1860) and elsewhere.

W103. *The People's Tune Book: a class book of church music for choirs, congregations, and singing schools.* New York: Mason Brothers, 1860; Boston: Crosby, Nichols, Lee & Co.; Philadelphia: J.B. Lippincott & Co., and E.H. Butler & Co.; Cincinnati: W.B. Smith & Co.; Chicago: Root & Cady, 1860.

About 17 X 25 cm. 304 pages. SATB, a mixture of open and close score. Music elements section aphoristic, not question-and-answer format, with music examples and exercises. The tunebook itself begins with "Old Hundred" (p. 31).

Music in various common meters. Editor indicates that the tunes found in *The Sabbath Hymn and Tune Book* (1859), W101, are included, "together with such tunes as were needed to supply meters not found in that work." Tunes are simple and easy. The preface denounces "difficult, florid, ornamented, highly artificial song."

1861

W104. *Asaph, or The Choir Book: a collection of vocal music, sacred and secular, for choirs, singing schools, musical societies and conventions, and social and religious assemblies.* New York: Mason Brothers, 1861.

Co-editors: Lowell Mason and William Mason

17 X 25 cm. 384 pages. Vocal exercises, Anglican chants, Psalm and hymn tunes, anthems, motets, canons, rounds, some occasional pieces. SATB without accompaniment. Open and close score.

Asaph was an Old Testament musician and poet, a Levite who led choral services established by King David. Mason had previously used the name in *Songs of Asaph* (1843), W64.

Many meters are used in the hymn tunes to accommodate commonly used texts. Anthems range from short and simple to long and complex. Under "Set Pieces, or Tunes of Particular Adaptation," the editors give "hymns of such peculiar meters as are not found in the ordinary hymn books." These are meant for "social religious occasions and home circles," not worship, because they are "generally touching, quickening, and enlivening." The central purpose of the book was to present music which "seemed to connect a dignified simplicity with strength of character, purity of style, and elegance of diction."

1863

W105. "Christ Hath Arisen." A Carol for Easter-Day, by Rev. E.A. Washburn, D.D. Music by Dr. Lowell Mason. New York: Mason Brothers, 1863.

> 16 cm. Total of 14 measures of SATB, chordal writing. Four stanzas, no refrain. Close score.

1864-66

W106. *The Song-Garden.* A series of school music books, progressively arranged. Each book complete in itself. First Book, New York: Mason Brothers, 1864; Boston: O. Ditson & Co., 1864. Second Book, New York: Mason Brothers, 1864; Boston: O. Ditson & Co., 1864. Third Book, New York: Mason Brothers, 1866; Boston: O. Ditson, 1866.

> Lowell Mason's only progressively graded series comparable to modern textbook series; the first graded series of song books for American school children. (See B137, B138, and B140)

> Oblong, 160 pages. Volumes vary in size. Songs from French, Spanish, German, English, Swiss and American sources. Writing in 2, 3, and 4 parts. No accompaniment. A few rounds, chants, hymn settings, but mostly short (one-page) strophic songs.

> Book I: "Elements" section is brief and elementary. "For a more complete course, both theoretical and practical, see *The Song-Garden*, Book II." Book III reviews the elements and includes an article on "vocal culture" plus canons and fughettas for 1, 2, and 3 voices.

> The plan of the series is elaborated in the preface to the first book. Each book is self-contained; each provides both music and text material. The books contain much material new to the American public.

1866

W107. *The New Sabbath Hymn and Tune Book for the Service of Song in the House of the Lord.* Boston: O. Ditson & Co., 1866.

> Same co-editors, format, and preface as *The Sabbath Hymn and Tune Book* (1859), W101, plus a new one-page preface. Some change in the tunes chosen. (B210, 171)

1868

W108. "Duty's Call." Parting song of the class of 1868, State Normal School, Westfield, Massachusetts. n.p., n.d.

> 35 cm., one oversized page. Text by Sadie E. Owen, beginning "Softly close the shades of twilight." SATB unaccompanied. Strophic, four stanzas, refrain, coda.

1869

W109. *Carmina Sacra Enlarged. The American Tune Book: a complete collection of the tunes which are widely popular in America, with the most popular anthems and set pieces, preceded by a new course of instruction for singing schools, by Dr. Lowell Mason. The tunes selected from all sources by five hundred teachers and choir leaders.* Boston: O. Ditson & Co., 1869.

> 17 X 24 cm. 440 pages. SATB, mostly unaccompanied chants, anthems with and without solo passages, glees, canons, motets, hymn and Psalm tunes. Uses three staves: top for tenor, middle for soprano/alto, bottom for bass line.

> About a thousand experienced teachers and choir leaders all over the United States were asked to indicate their favorite works. About five hundred responded, and from their lists the most popular works were selected. (Publisher's Notice)

W110. *Congregational Church Music: (Compressed Score Edition) A Book for the Service of Song in the House of the Lord. Containing Tunes, Chants and Anthems.* Arranged by John Goss, Esq., Dr. Lowell Mason, Mrs. M. Bartholomew, H.E. Dibdin, Esq., Rev. W.H. Havergal, M.A., E.J. Hopkins, Esq., the Late Wm Horsley, Esq., V. Novello, Esq., James Turle, Esq., and Others. London: Unwin Brothers, 1869.

> 15.5 X 12.5 cm. 142 pages. Contains 300 hymn tunes and 46 chants, no texts. Sources clearly stated. Also 45 anthems with texts, mostly chordal (more like sentences or responses). Close score, SATB.

> Bound with *Psalms and Hymns from Holy Scripture, Arranged for Chanting.* Contains 67 texts, plus some for chants. Total of 32 pages.

W111. *The Elements of Music and Its Notation, After the Interrogatory Manner.* Boston: O. Ditson & Co., 1869.

> A revision of the "Elements" section in *The Song-Garden*, Book III (1866), W106, and *Carmina Sacra Enlarged: The American Tune Book* (1869), W109. Essentially the same work was reissued in 1871 under the title *Elements of Music, Presented in the Form of Interrogation.* (New York: C.H. Ditson & Co.)

W112. "Our Labor Here Is Done." Parting song for the class of February 1869, State Normal School, Westfield, Massachusetts. n.p., n.d.

> 17 X 25 cm., one short page. SAB with no accompaniment. Very simple. Text by Lotta L. Noyes.

1870

W113. "With Loving Favor Crowned." Song of Farewell for the graduating class, February, 1870, State Normal School, Westfield, Massachusetts. n.p., n.d.

25 cm. Short, strophic SAB composition with a coda on "Farewell! Farewell!" Text by Harriet E. Leonard.

UNDATED

W114. "Christmas Carol." Words by Marie Mason (Mrs. Lowell Mason, Jr.) n.p., n.d.

Believed to be one of Lowell Mason's compositions. (B228, 171, n. 62). 30 cm. Strophic unaccompanied, one-page composition.

W115. Four Chants: "Psalm 100"; "Song of Moses at the Red Sea"; "Elegy of David"; "135th Psalm." n.p., n.d.

Believed to have been among Lowell Mason's compositions. (B228, 171, n. 62)

22 cm., seven-page folder. Modern format. Anglican chants with 2, 3, or 4 sections.

W116. "How Beautiful Upon the Mountains." n.p., n.d.

Believed to be one of Lowell Mason's compositions. (B228, 171, n. 62).

28 X 25 cm. 2 pages. Music for one to four voices and instruments. No poets or arrangers named.

W117. "I Love the Lord." (a quadruple chant). "He That Dwelleth" (a double chant). n.p., n.d.

Believed to have been among Lowell Mason's publications. (B228, 171, n. 62)

18 X 26 cm. As indicated in the titles.

W118. "Ode: Again the Voice of God." Words by Grenville Mellen. n.p., n.d.

13 X 26 cm. SATB, unaccompanied. Preceded by an "Ode" by G.J. Webb to a text by Park Benjamin. Both odes written in memory of John Marshall, Chief Justice of the Supreme Court, 1801-1835. Mason's work is four pages long; open score.

W119. "On Thy Church, O Power Divine." n.p., n.d.

15 X 26 cm., 2 pages. SATB, unaccompanied. Open score. Two stanzas and a coda. Text from *Church Psalmody* (1831), W9, "Ps. 67, 5th Pt."

W120. "Sentence: Come Unto Me." Written for the Light Street Choir, Baltimore, at the request of C. Tiffany, by his friend L. Mason. n.p., n.d.

SATB, 3 pages, unaccompanied. Some portions for individual sections alone, alternating with full choir.

W121. Tunes printed separately: "Aulis" (double choir); "Bright Source of Everlasting Love"; "Come Brothers"; "Pilgrim Song"; "Press Forward"; "The Little Pilgrims." n.p., n.d.

Believed to have been among Mason's publications. (B228, 171, n. 62). Various sizes and various styles. Some are numbered as though they had been in an anthology; some have holes on the edges where they could have been stitched into a book. These may be proof pages or pages which fell out of books.

W122. "Wedding Hymn: Now the Sacred Seal." Words by Ray Palmer. Boston: A. Wright, n.d.

18 X 26 cm. SATB, 4 pages unaccompanied though the opening solo has an instrumental bass line. Echo effects between the men's and women's voices. Sentimental text ending, "Heaven in kindness bless the pair, Lasting happiness bestow; Guide them safe to pastures where/Love's eternal waters flow."

Bibliography

Writings by Lowell Mason

The entries in this listing set forth Mason's views independent of his prefaces, introductions, elements sections of textbooks, and other writings incorporated within published works. The items listed below were published separately and served purposes independent of other publications.

Entries in the Catalog of Works above include comments about prefatory writings only when Mason's remarks are significant or exceptional in some way, or when those remarks help characterize the work. In the absence of any comments about prefatory sections, it is assumed that those writings serve the expected purposes, but that little out-of-the-ordinary content is to be found there.

The Catalog of Works includes not only his textbooks, tunebooks, hymnals, and sheet music, but also books such as the *Manual of the Boston Academy of Music* (1834), W20, a work of pedagogy and music examples for music teachers, and *Church Psalmody* co-edited with Greene (1831), W9, a book of texts for congregational singing. A few works seem to belong both in that catalog and in this listing, as, for instance, the *Manual of the Boston Academy of Music*. Because of its significance, that particular work is included both places, but with annotation in the catalog above. Normally a given work appears only once, in the one listing into which it more appropriately fits.

Many of the items listed below can be seen as by-products of Mason's career. The first two entries, for instance, were developed as presentations before church groups: a formal speech in 1826 and informal remarks at a social gathering in 1851. Certain publications were developed as revised versions of articles in periodicals, as, for example, *Musical Letters from Abroad* (1853), B7. In those instances, the original versions are not listed and annotated because the substance is reflected in the final published form.

* * * * * * * * * * *

B1. *Address on Church Music: Delivered by Request, on the Evening of Saturday, October 7, 1826, in the Vestry of Hanover Church, and on the Evening of Monday Following in the Third Baptist Church, Boston.* Boston: Hilliard, Gray & Company, 1826. Reprint. *The Choral and Organ Guide* (December 1965, January 1966, February 1966).

> Sets forth Mason's basic philosophy about styles of music appropriate for worship. Calls for congregational singing, capable choirs, and judicious use of instruments. "Children must be taught music as they are taught to read. Until something of this kind is done, it is vain to expect any great and lasting improvement." (B210, 40-42)

B2. *An Address on Church Music, Delivered July 8, 1851, in Boston.* New York: Mason & Law, 1851.

> Summarizes church music in America, particularly in Boston during his nearly twenty-five years there. Presented at his farewell party. (B210, 136)

B3. *A Brief Presentation of the Elementary Principles of Music, in Perceptive or Didactic Form.* New York: C.H. Ditson & Co., 1871.

Seems to be a revision of *The Elementary Principles of Vocal Music*, published with *The Song-Book of the School Room* (1847), W76. Designed for an introduction to the Pestalozzian approach to teaching; meant for use in schools.

B4. *A Glance at Pestalozzianism: Delivered Before the American Institute of Instruction in New Haven.* New York: Mason Brothers, 1863.

Seeks to inspire as well as explain his views of Pestalozzianism. Gives credit to Pestalozzi and Woodbridge for their contributions. Quotes Sir William Hamilton: "The highest end of education is not exertion; since the mind is not invigorated, developed, in a word *educated,* by the mere possession of truths, but by the energy determined in their quest and contemplation." Outlines his interpretation of Pestalozzian principles in ten main points.

B5. *How Shall I Teach? or, Hints to Teachers on the Use of Music and Its Notation.* New York: Mason Brothers, 1860. Reprint. Boston: O. Ditson Co., 1903.

Ten-page summary of Mason's ideas about teaching. Published in a pamphlet of about thirty pages with music lessons and exercises. Written to be included in G.F. Root's book *The Diapason* (1860) but printed separately first. (See pages 187-92 below.)

B6. *Manual of the Boston Academy of Music, for Instruction in the Elements of Vocal Music, on the System of Pestalozzi.* Boston: Carter, Hendee & Co., 1834.

Most thorough presentation of the methods Mason advocated. Contains general observations in opening chapters, then specific steps for teaching music reading. See B74, B212 for discussion of sources and content.

B7. *Musical Letters from Abroad: Including Detailed Accounts of the Birmingham, Norwich, and Dusseldorf Musical Festivals of 1852.* Boston: O. Ditson & Co., 1853. Reprint. New York: Da

Capo Press, 1967, with a new introduction by Elwyn A. Wienandt.

> Contains fifty-four informal essays on church music, concerts, festivals, and private meetings with musicians. Meant "to serve as a remembrance...to pupils and friends" and "to influence...those who were exerting themselves for [musical] improvement." (preface, iv) Reveals Mason's thinking on many topics and shows his skill as a critic, particularly of church music.

B8. "On Teaching Music."*The Choral Advocate and Singing Class Journal.* Part 1: 1 (June 1850): 8-9; Part 2: 1 (July 1850): 25.

> Reflects on changes in texts and approaches over a quarter century (c. 1825-1850). "Teaching is now acknowledged to be an art; it is no longer enough to have a mere knowledge of a subject...but in addition...the art of teaching....Perhaps the particular point in which the modern improved mode of teaching differs from those which prevailed a few years since, is this: the pupil is now taught to think...." Part 2 contrasts the "preceptive" and the "inductive" approaches to show the superiority of the latter.

B9. "The Pestalozzian Method of Teaching Music." *The Musical World and Times* 11, no. 2 (May 14, 1853): 22-23.

> Originally presented to a teachers' association in London and reported in the London *Musical World*. Summarizes what Pestalozzian method does *not* consist of, then what it does consist of, not in specific pedagogy so much as in effects upon the pupil: "to awaken the powers of the mind, to quicken and direct [him] aright...to place him upon the right track of investigation...and to cause him steadily and perseveringly to press onward...." (23)

B10. *The Pestalozzian Music Teacher: Or Class Instructor in Elementary Music, in Accordance with the Analytic Method.* To which are added illustrative lessons on form, number and arithmetic, language and grammar, and other school topics by John W. Dickinson, Principal of the State Normal School, Westfield, Mass. New York: C.H. Ditson & Co., 1871.

A 308-page volume prepared by Mason with the help of T.F. Seward. Most of the material had appeared in serial version in the *New York Musical Review and Gazette* (1855-1857). Offers a step-by-step presentation of all the topics covered in his "Elements" sections; gives questions to be asked by teachers, providing a kind of script to be followed in music teaching. Presents alternate explanations of some points. Includes some musical lessons, exercises, and short songs.

B11. *Song in Worship, an Address, With an Introduction by the Reverend Reuen Thomas.* Boston: Marvin & Son, 1878.

The exact date when this work was written is not known, but it appears to be one of Mason's later works. Sums up his attitudes about the importance of music in worship, attitudes also reflected in his earlier addresses and writings.

Songs in worship "should not be regarded as mere appendages, incidentals, or as condiments to the sermon; they are forms of worship, and they should be made acts of real worship in which every one should engage." (9) The only justification for singing in public worship is "as a religious act, or for a religious purpose, or for the promotion of religious growth. For this ONLY may we introduce singing into the house of the Lord." (12)

Writings About Lowell Mason

All the works listed below are annotated from the standpoint of what they add to an understanding of Lowell Mason's life and era or how they facilitate research into these and related topics. Direct quotations and paraphrases are followed by page citations. The quotations were selected for their style and capacity for suggesting what readers will find in the sources. Code numbers refer to codes within this book; numbers following the code numbers are page references.

* * * * * * * * * * *

B12.   Abbott, Jacob. "Lowell Mason at the Mt. Vernon School." *The Congregationalist*, August 22, 1875.

> Recalls this private school in the 1830s as a large building where about a hundred pupils sat in one large room, their desks arranged in rows according to students' ages (ranging from about 10-20). The pupils all learned together, no matter their background. Mason had to devise lessons to "be within the comprehension and the capabilities of the mere children, and at the same time so diversified, by the tact and ingenuity of the teacher, and by his power of interesting the pupils in principles which could be exemplified and illustrated by simple means, as to be made attractive to the most advanced."
>
> Describes Mason's sensitive handling of the class the day after the funeral of one of the students, Martha Jane Crockett, for whom "Mt. Vernon" was written.

B13. Alcott, W.A., M.D. "William Channing Woodbridge." *The American Journal of Education* 5, no. 8 (June 1858): 51-64.

> Describes Woodbridge's home, precocious youth (including his college degree earned before age 17), his "latent scrofula" and lifelong dyspepsia, his travels, his career as a writer, pioneer educator, and geographer. Points out Woodbridge's nervous weakness, but great

mental powers and moral endowments "still more eminent." Woodbridge was frugal to the point of parsimony with himself but "liberal to nobility" on behalf of educational and other benevolent causes in which he believed. (61)

In August 1831 Woodbridge purchased the journal he named the *Annals of Education* (Boston) and devoted himself in its first two years to writing "in a clear, careful, and faithful manner, the whole system of Fellenberg; together with such other systems of distinguished European educators as were meritorious, particularly those of Pestalozzi at Yverdun and Prof. Jacotot of Louvain...." (59)

Excellent source for insight into this major figure in Mason's career, yet concerning Mason, Alcott is in error: for instance, "He [Woodbridge] drew from behind the counter of a country store and introduced into the higher sphere in which he has done so great and useful a work, the celebrated Lowell Mason...." (63)

B14.   American Institute of Instruction. *The Introductory Discourse and the Lectures Delivered Before the American Institute of Instruction in Boston, August,1833. Including a List of Officers and Members.* Boston: Carter, Hendee and Co., 1834.

Proceedings, Introductory lecture by William Sullivan, plus ten lectures on various subjects, including "On the Necessity of Educating Teachers" by Samuel R. Hall and "On the Classification of Schools" by Samuel M. Burnside. Gives insight into methods, practices, and problems of concern to Mason and other educators of the day. Comparable volumes were published for other years.

B15.   "American Musical Literature." *The Musical Reporter* 1, no. 2 (February 1841): 62-65.

Assesses contemporary music books, including several by Mason. Criticizes the duplication of materials: "From three fourths to seven eighths of the tunes in most of these books with some alterations are common to them all." (64) Highly critical of compositions of the day.

B16.   Austin, William W. *"Susanna," "Jeanie," and "The Old Folks at Home": The Songs of Stephen C. Foster from His Time to Ours*. New York: Macmillan, 1975. Revised edition. Urbana: University of Illinois Press, forthcoming 1987 or 1988.

> Shows Mason's contemporaries, including songwriters G.F. Root and Foster, absorbing Mason's idioms and, in Root's words, finding their own expression after having "imbibed more of Dr. Mason's spirit." The chapter entitled "'People's Song' Writers Following Foster" is particularly relevant to Mason's influence.

> Demonstrating that influence concretely, the author compares "Susanna" in its form and melodic line with Mason's "Missionary Hymn." "The resemblance might be mere coincidence, or it might point to some earlier common source, but probably Foster had absorbed Mason's melody from the singing of his mother and sisters; now he fused its firm shape of pitches with the new [polka] rhythm and the comic words." (10)

> Thorough indexing and extensive, often discursive notes. A book full of insight into "historical and cultural issues that can be related to Mason's work even if he has slipped over the horizon....the pages about Foster's own hymns could find better readers among experts on Mason than in some other circles." (William W. Austin in a letter to the writer, September 2, 1987)

B17. Axley, Lowry. *Holding Aloft the Torch: A History of the Independent Presbyterian Church of Savannah, Georgia*. Savannah: The Pigeonhole Press, 1958.

> Describes the church in which young Lowell Mason played significant roles during his Savannah years (1813-1827). Shows Mason's part in building its musical and educational programs.

B18. Ayars, Christine Merrick. *Contributions to the Art of Music in America by the Music Industries of Boston, 1640 to 1936*. New York: The H. W. Wilson Company, 1937.

> Based on a master's thesis, but expanded into a valuable reference work. Data on music journals alone would make the book valuable, but the information on early printing and engraving, music publishers, and instrument manufacturers is also useful. Mason &

Hamlin described, though mainly covering the decades after Lowell Mason's life. Well-indexed.

B19. Bacon, George Blagden. "Exercises at the Opening of the Lowell Mason Library of Music in the Yale Divinity School, May 11, 1875: An Address." New Haven, n.p., 1875.

Praises Lowell Mason for his contribution to church music in America. Bacon was Mason's clergyman and friend during his last years in Orange, NJ.

B20. ------. "Lowell Mason." *Congregational Quarterly* 15, no. 1 (January 1873): 1-15.

Reflects on the state of church music in New England before Mason's time and on Mason's lack of formal training: "How well he did it [his work] we shall hardly appreciate unless we remember with what slender resources he wrought. For he had no advantages of education, as almost to his latest day, he regretfully remembered....[As] the New-England boys of that day had to, he began almost in the cradle that fight for a living which left small opportunity for study and for culture." (7)

Praises Mason: "Always striving to perfect himself in his profession, he was resolute by every means to perfect others also." (9) Also mentions that Mason was resolute in working for his goals in the schools and the churches; adds that the churches owe more to Mason than they realize because many of Mason's musical works were first published unsigned, and some of them were never claimed. (15)

B21. ------. *Sermon, Commemorative of Lowell Mason.* N.Y.: Cushing, Bardua & Co., 1872.

Twenty-two page tribute, mainly praising Mason for his contributions to church music. Begins with a bleak picture of church music before Mason's time: "a scant catalogue of five or six sedate and decent tunes with which, down to the year 1770, or thereabouts, the churches were content to worship."

Indicates that Mason's publishing changed that picture. The first edition of the *Boston Handel and Haydn Society Collection* not only paid for itself within a year and after seven or eight editions made the society "ten thousand dollars richer for its patronage of the young author," but also "arrested the evil tendency of church music in New England, and turned the tide in the direction of a simple, decorous and scientific style. With the publication of this volume the days of the preposterous and pyrotechnic style of psalm-tunes were already numbered." (14)

Praises Mason's industry: "he would scarcely have completed one book before he was eager to produce another and a better." (14) Also for his character: says former pupils attest to the "moral tone which his character imparted to their lives." (17) "It was the fact that he was teachable himself, that fitted him to be a teacher of others....[He was] never too old to learn." (21)

B22. Baldwin, Sister Mary F.X. "Lowell Mason's Philosophy of Music Education." M.A. thesis, Catholic University of America, 1937.

Examination of Mason's writing on education and a summary of the "ultimate aims" and "secondary aims" of music education as indicated in Mason's philosophy. Introductory, basic but well-written.

B23. Baltzel, Winton James. "A Picture of Community Music Work Eighty Years Ago." *The Musician* 22, no. 12 (December 1917): 897.

Baltzel, editor of *The Musician* (a publication of O. Ditson, Co.) based this article on a conversation with "the late L.O. Emerson, born 1820 in Parsonfeld, Me."

Describes notice of a singing school, c. 1830-35. For $1.50 tuition for 24 lessons, students will learn note reading. "Bring Lowell Mason's book." Notice gave local youth "pleasant anticipations of social diversion...merriment and good times as well as learning to sing from note, thus qualifying for a place in the choir to be organized later."

Describes the schoolhouse with pupils carrying lanterns to their lessons. Rudiments taught with "do, re, mi" and pupils learning "time-
beating" by doing hand motions. "By the time the last lesson was
reached these young people had learned to read from note with
some facility, and were generally accurate in time; the usual hymn
tunes of the period could be learned readily enough. Of real training
in singing there was little or none....[Yet] the old-fashioned singing
school was...useful...and kept alive in the hearts of the people a love
for music and a desire for its cultivation which laid a good foundation
for its later progress."

B24. *Boston Academy of Music Reports.* Boston: Perkins &
Marvin, 1833-1846.

Primary sources, though somewhat self-serving in the manner typical
of annual reports. Factual data presumably reliable. Attitudes and
stated objectives as important as factual data, if not more so. Significant portions reprinted in B272.

B25. Boston Academy of Music. *Programmes of Concerts. May
15, 1833-February 27, 1845.* Boston Public Library, 1833-1845.

Excellent information, a reflection of performance capabilities
through the repertoire and a means of deducing the academy's musical influence.

B26. Barnard, Henry. "Educational Labors of Lowell Mason."
The American Journal of Education 4 (1857): 141-48.

Complimentary summary by a prominent contemporary. "Dr. Mason
owes his high reputation...to the fact that he has pursued his long and
arduous career as a teacher...on broad and generous principles
elevated far above all barely technical or mechanical skill....[His] influence...has been in the highest degree conducive to the cultivation
of *purity of taste*...." (146-47) Cites Horace Mann's comment that it
was "well worth any young teacher's while to walk ten miles to hear a
lecture by Dr. Mason; for in it he would hear a most instructive exposition of the true principles of all teaching, as well as that of instruction in music." (146)

More specific observations on Mason's teaching: his "rare tact in developing the vital principles of instruction in the simplest and happiest manner, his endless variety of illustrations, his indefatigable perseverance in teaching and exposing errors in thought or in theory, his genial and humane humor, his playful sallies of wit, his kindly sympathy to youth and childhood, his gentle yet impressive monitory hints, and occasional grave reflections, gave him an indescribable power over his audience; while the perfect simplicity and strictly elementary character of his instruction evince the depths to which he has penetrated, in tracing the profoundest philosophy of teaching." (146)

B27. Benson, Louis F. *The English Hymn: Its Development and Use in Worship.* Richmond: John Knox Press, 1962.

Only scattered references to Mason, yet helpful in placing Mason's role as hymn writer/editor in context. Traces development of American hymns and hymnals, showing Mason's part in moving toward modern hymnals, particularly with respect to his work with Andover professors Park and Phelps. (475ff.)

B28. Benton, Rita. "Early Musical Scholarship in the United States." *Fontes* 11, no. 1 (January-April 1964): 12-21.

Deals with Mason's library, built to become a "public benefit" after his death. Some details on the Thayer/Mason association.

B29. Beuchner, Alan Clark. "Yankee Singing Schools and the Golden Age of Choral Music in New England, 1760-1800." Ed.D. diss., Harvard University, 1960.

B30. Birge, Edward Bailey. *History of Public School Music in the United States.* Boston: Oliver Ditson Co., 1928. Reprint. Washington, D.C.: Music Educators National Conference, 1966.

Classic reference, providing the context for Mason and his era. Fulfills the author's purposes: "to rescue from oblivion certain aspects of public school music which are becoming legendary...to describe merely the main trend of the evolution of public school music, and to

account as far as possible for the direction this evolution has taken."
(Preface) Brief bibliography; illustrations; readable style.

B31. ------. "One Hundred Years of School Music." *Music Educators Journal* 22, no. 1 (September 1935): 19.

Cites the significance of Mason's public school teaching in Boston:
the fact that "the Boston school fathers had the courage to vote the
privilege [music instruction] to *all* the children at *public expense*...made school boards everywhere wait upon the success of the
experiment before following the example...." In error about Mason's
career in the Boston schools after 1838; Mason did not resign after
three years "so as to travel about and 'help the cause.'"

B32. Blackburn, David Stuart. "The Life, Works, and Songs of
Richard Storrs Willis." D.M.A. diss., University of Iowa, 1971.

Part of a performance project in solo song literature; includes a short
biography of Willis (1819-1900). Perhaps his greatest influence was
through editing *The Musical World and New York Musical Times*, a
journal which helped promote the Mason/Root/Bradbury musical institutes in the 1850s. Lists Willis' known works and evaluates his
songs as "excellent in construction."

B33. Bode, Carl, ed. *American Life in the 1840s*. New York:
Anchor Books, 1967.

Concise overview of domestic, economic, and intellectual life of the
period. On Mason, "the nation's choirmaster," (239) brief but accurate.

B34. ------. *The Anatomy of American Popular Culture, 1840-
1861*. Los Angeles: University of California Press, 1959.

Provides insight into attitudes about religion, morality, education,
and popular entertainment during the height of Mason's career.
Helps in understanding Mason's attitudes about text selection and
roles of music in people's lives. Includes brief but perceptive description of Mason's work.

B35. Brandon, George. "Some Classic Tunes in Lowell Mason Collections." *The Hymn* 18, no. 3 (1967): 78-79.

> Identifies about twenty chorale tunes, twenty psalm tunes, and two pre-Reformation tunes of the 16th and 17th centuries in the *New Carmina Sacra* (1850), W85, *Cantica Laudis* (with Webb, 1850), W82, and *Carmina Sacra Enlarged: The American Tune Book* (1869), W109. Raises the question of whether Mason put these tunes into his books because they were already popular or whether he was partly responsible for their popularity through his publications.

B36. Brayley, A.W. "The Inception of Public School Music in America." *The Musician* 10 (November 1905): 483-85.

> Provides information about Joseph Harrington, Jr. and Hawes Grammar School in Boston prior to Mason's teaching there. Offers details of the Boston School Committee's work in the 1830s.

B37. Brayley, George. "Early Instrumental Music in Boston." *The Bostonian* 1 (November 1894): 189-96.

> Describes chapel organs, stringed instruments, flutes, oboes, and pitch pipes used in churches during the 1700s and concerts of the 1780s and 1790s in Boston. Indicates the scarcity of instruments and instrumental musicians during the early years of Mason's life.

B38. Britton, Allen P. "Music Education: An American Specialty." *Music Educators Journal* 48 (June/July 1962): 27-29, 55-63. Republished in *Perspectives in Music Education: Source Book III* (Washington, D.C.: MENC, 1966), 15-28.

> Attempts to "explain something of the intellectual climate within which music educators have been obliged...to pursue their careers." (18) Assesses the impulse toward "better music," including Mason's efforts to "find understandable music that could be taken as 'classical.'" (18) Valuable insight into Mason's work and attitudes and their place in music education history.

B39.   ------. "Music in Early American Public Education: A Historical Critique." *Basic Concepts in Music Education.* Chicago: University of Chicago Press, 1958.

> Summarizes music in North America from the time of Pedro de Gante (1523) through the singing schools and into Mason's era.

B40.   ------. "Theoretical Introductions in American Tune Books." Ph.D. diss., University of Michigan, 1949.

> Thorough, readable account that provides information about American books and methods pre-dating Mason and laying the foundation for his early training and work in music education.

> "The primary task of this study has been to explore and analyze the content of theoretical introductions to the American tune-book of the eighteenth century." (403) Results are set forth in two ways: discourse that discusses, compares and contrasts the material found; an annotated catalog of tunebooks. These tunebooks contain religious vocal music and were published in the U.S. before 1801 or after 1800 if the compilers had begun publishing before; thus the complete works of all 18th c. compilers appear. (472)

> The study encompasses "at least 319 separate editions, representing 152 individual titles of works." (120) The annotated listing includes publication information for separate editions as well as a description of contents. Valuable bibliography of secondary sources as well.

B41. Brooks, Henry M. *Olden-Time Music: A Compilation from Newspapers and Books.* Boston: Ticknor & Co., 1888.

> Concert programs and announcements from Boston and Salem to about 1830. Tells of H.K. Oliver's association with Mason with respect to the writing and publishing of "Federal Street." Reflects on church choirs in the early 1800s: "Choristers...grew strong in vanity and conceit, ...introducing 'flashy anthems, boisterous fuguing choruses, and long-spun-out solos.' The choirs gradually became very important, and began to claim privileges." (212) Little pertains to Lowell Mason directly, but the material reveals the musical climate of his early years.

B42. Broyles, Michael. "Lowell Mason on European Church Music and Transatlantic Cultural Identification: A Reconsideration." *Journal of the American Musicological Society* 38, no. 2 (1985): 316-48.

> Well-documented discussion of Mason's 1837 European trip based on analysis of Mason's travel diaries. Appendices include a listing of churches Mason visited and a long quote from Mason's diary, an account of the concert at Linchen Erben. Deals with the Mason-Neukomm relationship and Mason's reasons for the 1837 trip. Assesses Mason's views of American music and his detailed observations of corresponding developments abroad.

> Contains many insights: e.g., "Mason did not need to turn American musical taste back to Europe because it had never left it in the first place; and the very idea that he needed to do so...would have probably been inexplicable to him. Mason viewed American music as part of a single Anglo-American culture. In his eyes, the essential cultural distinction was between English-speaking and other Continental cultures." (333) As a church music reformer, Mason addressed problems similar to those found in England, and his solutions were "similar to those of British reformers. In spite of their German tinge, his models were as British in origin as those of William Billings." (342)

B43. Buffaloe, Bonnie Gail. "The Pestalozzianism of Lowell Mason: Its Identification and Importance to the Development of American Music Education During the Nineteenth Century." M.A. thesis, University of Denver, 1974. 76 pp.

B44. Burnham, Collins G. "Olden Time Music in the Connecticut Valley." *New England Magazine* 24 (March 1901): 12-27.

> Detailed, illustrated discussion of New England church music in the decades just before Mason. Surveys changes in attitudes from about 1720 to 1820. Shows influences of clergy, such as Jonathan Edwards and Samuel Willard, and tunebook compilers, such as Timothy Swann and Solomon Warriner, on church music tastes and practices.

B45. Carder, Mazie Pauline. "George Frederick Root, Pioneer Music Educator: His Contributions to Mass Instruction in Music." Ed.D. diss., University of Maryland, 1971.

> Rich source of biographical and bibliographical data on Root. Lists his publications; describes his teaching career and methods. Important for comparison with Mason's work and for understanding relationships between these contemporaries.

B46. Chase, Gilbert. "America's Music: The First Century." *The American Music Teacher* 26, no. 1 (September/October 1976): 10-13, 18.

> Describes American popular music and its composers during Mason's era, including Fry, Heinrich, Gottschalk, Root, Foster, and others. Conveys the sense that popularity meant "personal involvement permeating all classes," (13) a sense that Mason understood and capitalized upon.

B47. ------. *America's Music from the Pilgrims to the Present.* 3rd ed. Urbana: The University of Illinois Press, 1987.

> Readable account placing Mason and his era in context. Understandable to general readers as well as historians. Extensive but selective bibliography.

> Concerning a previous edition, but still applicable: "Chase offers a perspective in which American music is shown to have values different from, rather than inferior to, European music — values in which the center of gravity is found in popular rather than in so-called serious musical forms." Richard Crawford, *American Studies and American Musicology: A Point of View and a Case in Point* (Brooklyn, NY: ISAM, 1975), 3.

B48. Cheney, Simeon Pease. *The American Singing Book, Contains More Than 300 Pages of a Great Variety of Excellent Sacred and Secular Music, Old and New...[with] Biographies of Forty of the Leading Composers, Book-makers, etc. of Sacred Music in America, from William Billings to I.B. Woodbury, which alone is worth the price of the book.* Boston: White, Smith and Company, 1879. Reprint New York: Da Capo Press, 1980 with introductory remarks by H. Wiley Hitchcock and Karl Kroeger.

> Contains a brief interpretive biography with anecdotes not found elsewhere. Recalls he heard Mason sing, though he was not known as a singer. Demonstrating a song at a convention, Mason sang "in a more natural and pleasing manner than I had...ever before or have ever since heard it sung." (192) Quotes a letter from Mason dated Jan. 12, 1865; Mason reflects on how little value he sees in writing an autobiography, says that he would probably not create another church music book, and deplores the "trashy...wretched Sunday-school books" being issued.(193)

B49. Clark, Frances. "School Music in 1836, 1886, 1911, and 1936." *NEA Proceedings* (1924): 603-11.

> Puts Mason's educational work in perspective. Interesting as evidence of how Mason was viewed in the early twentieth century.

B50. "Convention of Teachers of Vocal Music." *American Annals of Education* 6 (October 1836): 473-74.

> Lists the resolutions passed at the August 1836 teachers' convention in Boston, including resolutions about improving church music and adding vocal music to the school curricula.

B51. Cook, Wanda V. "Methodology in Public School Music: A Survey of Changes in the Aims and Procedures of Music Teaching in the Public Schools of the United States During the Past One Hundred Years." M.M. thesis, Michigan State University, 1939.

> Recognizes Mason and his followers' efforts to establish an American conception of music as based on public involvement in homes, churches, and communities. Assesses Mason's role as a pioneer music educator.

B52. Cooke, Francis T., and others. *A Century of Service: 1860-1960. Historical Sketch of the Highland Avenue Congregational Church, Orange, New Jersey.* n.p., 1960.

> Commemorative booklet with details about the Mason family's involvement with the congregation and gifts presented in honor of Lowell Mason.

B53. Copeland, Robert M. "The Life and Works of Isaac Baker Woodbury, 1819-1858." Ph.D. diss., University of Cincinnati, 1974.

> Summary biography of Woodbury, a Mason student in the 1830s. Surveys his output: responsible for 700 compositions or publications in 16 years. Analysis of his 15 juvenile and adult tunebooks shows that his style closely resembles Mason's, though Woodbury composed a wider range of music, including 140 songs for voice and piano, 4 cantatas, 3 oratorios, and a music drama. Seven instrumental instruction books and a book of composition and harmony, like the other works, show Woodbury's philosophy parallels Mason's "American Pestalozzianism." Valuable study.

B54. Cranch, Christopher P. "Address Delivered Before the Harvard Musical Association, in the Chapel of the University at Cambridge, August 28, 1845." Boston: S.N. Dickinson & Co., 1845.

> Reflects on the "actual condition [of music] in our own country," saying that "in the science and art of music we Americans are as yet scarcely pupils, and of course far enough from being masters." (13) "What we all need, and what the young especially need, is the very best models to perfect their taste." (14) Goes on to argue for German music and for better American music criticism: "The rarest of all things is to find a person, who, to a thorough knowledge of the mechanical and material, unites a deep, hearty, intellectual feeling of the spiritual significance of music." (17) Echoes Mason or Mason echoes him, or both echo the thinking of the times.

B55. Crawford, Richard. "'Much Still Remains to Be Undone': Reformers of Early American Hymnody." *The Hymn* 35, no. 4 (1984): 204-8.

A line quoted from Mason's first tunebook (1822) sets the tone; Law, Mason, Hastings, and Bradbury shown to agree about styles of music suitable for church use. Shows Mason in step with other would-be church music reformers.

B56. -----. "Musical Learning in Nineteenth-Century America." *American Music* 1 (Spring 1983): 1-11.

Contrasts perspectives toward American music: as an extension of European culture vs. an outgrowth of musical developments in America. Mason's interpretation of musical learning involved "the summary rejection of uncultivated musics (and hence of most people's earlier experience and instinctive tastes), the commitment to change for 'improvement's' sake, and the particular amalgam of self-interest and morality that justified the process." (4) Shows how Mason's thinking fits into the context of his era.

B57. Cross, Virginia Ann. "The Development of Sunday School Hymnody in the United States of America, 1816-1869." D.M.A. diss., New Orleans Baptist Theological Seminary, 1985.

Well-documented, well-written study based on examination of the books themselves. Describes Mason's Sabbath School books individually with comparisons and contrasts between his books and those of others. Many music examples, often complete songs as originally published. Presents much valuable and hard-to-obtain material; carefully organized with clearly stated conclusions.

B58. Cubberly, Ellwood P. *Public Education in the United States.* New York: Houghton Mifflin, 1919.

Describes American experiments with Pestalozzian ideas by Woodbridge, Neef, and Griscom. Illustrated. Some documentation.

B59.   Damrosch, Frank. "Music in the Public Schools." *American History and Encyclopedia of Music*, W.L. Hubbard, ed. (New York: Irving Squire Toledo, 1908): 8: 17-37. Reprint. New York: AMS Press, 1976.

> Quotes objectives of the Boston Academy of Music, resolutions of the Boston School Committee in January 1832, parts of the Davis report of 1837, and advertisements for the academy's teachers' class (1839). Observes that "As a foundation for all musical study it is necessary to create the appreciation of the beautiful in sound and at the same time to make the child realize that music is intended as a vehicle for self-expression. The child learns these things by means of the rote song." (29) Reflects on the social values of music in the schools and mentions teachers' pay: "cities of from 8000 to 200,000 inhabitants usually employ only one special teacher of music, the salary ranging from $300 to $2500 per annum...." (35)

B60.   Dearing, Rachel. *Commemorative Booklet: Westborough's 250th Anniversary Committee*. Westborough, MA: n.p., 1967.

> Describes the community in which Abigail Gregory Mason grew up and provides basic information on her family. Illustrated, including a picture of the Gregory Inn.

B61.   Dichter, Harry and Elliott Shapiro. *Early American Sheet Music, Its Lure and Its Lore, 1768-1889*. New York: R.R. Bowker Co., 1941.

> Classifies sheet music by chronology and topic, offers a directory of early publishers, artists, and lithographers working on early sheet music, and provides 32 pages of facsimiles. Not as rewarding as one would hope about Mason's music, but the information that is offered is specific. Examples: lists four versions of "My Country, 'Tis of Thee" published between 1831 and 1861; cites Mason's connection with Sarah Josepha Hale's "Mary Had a Little Lamb," first published as a poem in 1830, then set to music and published in *The Juvenile Lyre* (Mason and Ives, 1831), W10.

B62. Dickey, Frances M. "The Early History of Public School Music in the United States." *Papers and Proceedings of the MTNA* (1914): 185-209.

> Detailed information about events in Boston in the 1830s. Quotes extensively from Woodbridge, the Davis Report of 1837, and School Committee resolutions. Summarizes ideas of Woodbridge, Harrington, and Mason. Offers details about the introduction of music in other cities, providing a basis for comparison with Boston, particularly four cities of Ohio—Columbus, Cleveland, Cincinnati, Toledo—"like a second New England because of their pronounced interest in all educational matters and their desire to improve church music." (203-204) Good bibliography.

B63. Doane, Frances. "The Influence of Pestalozzianism upon Lowell Mason's Work in Music Education. M.A. thesis, University of Vermont, 1937.

> Introductory material. Most useful portion is analysis of Mason's writings in light of Pestalozzian principles.

B64. Dooley, James Edward. "Thomas Hastings: American Church Musician." Ph.D. diss., Florida State University, 1963.

> Biographical study of Hastings with a catalog of his publications. Some information on the Mason/Hastings relationship. Shows that Mason's influence pervades anthologies of other musicians, that Mason and his contemporaries used works from one another freely, and that Mason's music was represented even in books which contained little American music overall.

B65. Doxey, Mary Bitzer. "Lowell Mason, Modern Music Educator." M.M. thesis, University of Mississippi, 1957.

> Correlates Mason's work with modern texts, often quite specifically. Yields little new information, but assimilates existing information well.

B66. Eaklor, Vicki L. "Music in American Society, 1815-1860: An Intellectual History." Ph.D. diss., Washington University, 1982.

> Intended to "conduct a comprehensive inquiry into the musical thought and activity of this relatively obscure era, and to detect what relationship, if any, existed between an American self-image and a musical culture that were forming simultaneously." (ii) Summarizes American music before 1815, then focuses on "Music and the Spirit of Reform," including chapters on sacred music, school music, transcendental musical thought, and music criticism.

> Affirms that Mason's work embodied the prevailing view that "the use of music in the moral education of Americans...was the essential foundation of the culture...." (156) Mason was "perhaps unique in his perception of two sets of ideals—musical and non-musical—that could coexist in the culture if not forced to cohabit. That it was Mason who introduced 'America,' at a children's celebration, now appears as notable as the song itself." (158) Well-documented, logically organized, and readable study; valuable for its breadth of investigation and interpretation.

B67. ------. "Roots of an Ambivalent Culture: Music, Education, and Music Education in Antebellum America." *Journal of Research in Music Education* 33, no. 2 (Summer 1985): 87-99.

> Confirms that Mason was a man of his times as a church music reformer and pioneer educator who emerged "from the tradition of New England psalmody [and] held views indistinguishable from those of the school reformers." (93) Summarizes American church music reform movements of earlier generations and the evolving role of music in the common schools: "if public education was partly a means of assuring the moral character and social responsibility of America's youth, then music was its natural ally; the cultivation of music for its sake...was secondary to its use as a means of social control in an era of instability...." (93) Shows that "music in the antebellum common school both typified and contributed to a uniquely American ambivalence between musical and amusical ideals that came to the hallmark of the culture." (87) Useful bibliography.

B68. Efland, Arthur. "Art and Music in the Pestalozzian Tradition." *Journal of Research in Music Education* 31, no. 3 (1983): 165-78.

> Shows Pestalozzian principles applied to art and music teaching. Assesses Mason's adaptations of sources; observes that "by 1830 Pestalozzianism was a generic term embracing a number of methods then current...." (175) Interesting comparisons and contrasts, art vs. music.

B69. Eliot, Samuel A. *Address Before the Boston Academy of Music on the Opening of the Odeon, August 5, 1835.* Boston: Perkins, Marvin & Co., 1835.

> Eloquent statement on music and its value, a revealing insight into Eliot's thinking. Available in modern sources, including B238 and B272. Eliot began twelve years as president of the academy in 1835; from 1836-1840 he was also the mayor of Boston.

B70. ------. "Mason's Address on Church Music: A Critical Review." *North American Review* 24 (January 1827): 244-46.

> Reviews Mason's address of October 7, 1826. Generally concurs with Mason but does not "see the propriety of charging this body [the church] with such a commission" as devising means of improving church music; rather, the duty should be "committed to...those who are best informed upon the subject [musicians]." (245) Repeats Mason's assertions that "wherever congregational singing has prevailed, there has been neither good tone, correct intonation, distinct articulation, nor proper emphasis or expression." (246)

B71. ------. "Music in America." *North American Review* 52 (April 1841): 320-38.

> "A great revolution in the musical character of the American people has begun, and is, we trust, to go forward....till its ultimate object be obtained." (320) Stresses the arguments favoring music, as a social enjoyment, pleasure, physical and intellectual exercise; connects good reading and singing.

Reviews the events leading to the instituting of music in the Boston schools, connecting efforts of the Boston Academy of Music with that development: "We consider this as the most important thing done by the Academy, or which can be done to promote the progress of music among us." (232) Speaks of the roles played by Woodbridge, Eliot, Mason, and Webb. Touches upon the rise of music magazines and quotes two full pages from the T.Kemper Davis Report of 1837.

B72.   Ellinwood, Leonard. *The History of American Church Music.* New York: Morehouse-Gorham Co., 1953.

Summarizes the use and handling of separate music books and psalters, tunebooks, and hymnals. (67-68) Succinct description of fuguing tunes: "an opening homophonic phrase followed by a polyphonic section using either strict or free imitation in at least three parts. This section is then followed by a concluding, homophonic phrase...." (29) Offers a rationale for printing practices. Only brief summaries of Mason and his contemporaries.

B73.   Ellis, Howard Eber. "The Influence of Pestalozzianism on Instruction in Music." Ph.D. diss., University of Michigan, 1957.

Purpose: "to determine to what extent the theory of education developed by Pestalozzi influenced music instruction in the schools to 1860." Traces Pestalozzian instruction in America before Mason and Mason's adaptations of Pestalozzianism over the years. Concludes that Mason never reached the point of believing the mass of American music teachers "grasped the real meaning of Pestalozzian theory" and that few teachers up to 1860 understood basic Pestalozzian principles though many adopted Pestalozzian methods.

B74.   ------. "Lowell Mason and the *Manual of the Boston Academy of Music.*" *Journal of Research in Music Education* 3 (Spring 1955): 3-10.

Comparison between Mason's book and G.F. Kübler's *Anleitung Zum Gesang-Unterrichte in Schulen.* Believes that Mason edited but did not write much of the *Manual* and that the *Manual*, like Kübler's work, was not essentially Pestalozzian in nature.

B75. Elson, Louis Charles. *The History of American Music*. rev. ed. New York: Macmillan, 1915.

> Illustrated. Brief description of Mason's life and career and those of his contemporaries. Topical organization.

B76. ------. *The National Music of America and Its Sources*. Boston: L.C. Page & Co. Inc., 1900.

> Attempts to trace the tune and texts for "My Country, 'Tis of Thee," first used in 1831 at a July 4 celebration at Park Street Church, Boston. Summary remarks about Mason's part in the Handel and Haydn Society, Boston Academy of Music, and music education.

B77. Fisher, Robert. "H. Theodore Hach and *The Musical Magazine*: A Historical Perspective." *Council for Research in Music Education Bulletin* 92 (Summer 1987): 35-46.

> Discusses the magazine, "the first scholarly journal concerned with the advancement of music education and public school music in America," (35) its editor, and the climate in which it appeared: Boston, January 1839-April 1842. Deals with the rift between Mason and Webb as reflected in the journal. Points to the tension between performance and pedagogy; in Hach's view, "both are equally important and necessary for the training of the 'good teacher.'" (45) Valuable information on little-known journals and figures of the period.

B78. Fisher, William Arms. *Music Festivals in the United States: An Historical Sketch*. Boston: The American Choral and Festival Alliance, Inc., 1934.

> Short chapter on Boston festivals, including the Peace Jubilees of 1869 and 1872. Describes the concerts of February 1815, celebrating the end of the War of 1812. Out of enthusiasm generated by the concerts, the Boston Handel and Haydn Society was organized on March 30, 1815; Mason's affiliation with the society began in 1821. The festival concerts of 1812 and 1815 featured parts of Haydn's

Creation and Handel's *Judas Maccabeus*, and Handel's *Ode to St. Cecilia's Day* and the *Dettingen Te Deum*.

B79. -----. *Notes on Music in Old Boston*. Boston: O. Ditson, 1918.

. Illustrated, lively history of the Ditson Company and the musical climate in which it grew, including Mason's years in Boston (1827-1851).

B80. -----. *One Hundred and Fifty Years of Music Publishing in the United States, 1783-1933: An Historical Sketch with Special Reference to the Pioneer Publisher, Oliver Ditson Co., Inc.* Boston: O. Ditson, 1933. Reprint. St. Clair Shores, MI: Scholarly Press, Inc., 1977.

A revised, expanded version of *Notes on Music in Old Boston.* Adds information about other music publishers in Boston and publishers in Baltimore, Philadelphia, New York, Cincinnati, and Chicago. Adds a little detail on the Musical Fund Society of the Boston Academy of Music: their orchestra ran eight concert seasons, succeeding the academy orchestra, with the last season in 1855.

B81. Flueckiger, Samuel Lehmann. "Lowell Mason's Contributions to the Early History of Music Education in the United States." Ph.D. diss., Ohio State University, 1936.

Rich source of information, biographical and bibliographical, factual and interpretive.

B82. ------. "Why Lowell Mason Left the Boston Schools." *Music Educators Journal* 22 (February 1936): 20-23.

Deals with the political upheaval in the fall of 1845. Detailed, well-documented account so far as it goes, but many questions about this episode remain unanswered.

B83. Foote, Henry Wilder. "Musical Life in Boston in the Eighteenth Century." *Proceedings of the American Antiquarian*

Society at the Annual Meeting Held in Worcester October 18, 1939. New Series 49/2 (1940).

> Noting that "Evidence has a way of escaping detection by those who never take the trouble to look for it," (297) the author examines the historical record concerning musical life in Puritan New England. Describes the controversies over singing "by rule" as opposed to singing "by rote," puts psalm singing into perspective as more musical than often supposed, and discusses the rise of tunebook publishing around 1800.

B84. ------. *Three Centuries of American Hymnody.* Cambridge, MA: Harvard University Press, 1940.

> Places Mason and his contemporaries in perspective as powerful influences on American hymnody and offers useful background for music education history: "If one were forced to select the one account which best tells the story behind the origin of vocal music instruction in the United States, he could do no better than to choose that given by...Foote in the first three chapters and the appendices of [this book]." (B40, 18).

B85. Fouts, Gordon E. "Music Instruction in America to Around 1830 as Suggested by the Hartzler Collection of Early Protestant American Tune-Books." Ph.D. diss., University of Iowa, 1968.

B86. ------. "Music Instruction in Early Nineteenth-Century American Monitorial Schools." *Journal of Research in Music Education* 22 (Summer 1974): 112-19.

> Explains the monitorial system, traces its history, and outlines its advantages and disadvantages as seen by H.K. Oliver and Horace Mann. Uses *Sabbath School Psalmody* (Ezra Barrett, 1830) as an example of a music text for monitorial schools. Background for understanding the work of Mason and other music educators in the early 1800s.

B87. ------. "Music Instruction in the Education of American Youth: The Early Academies." *Journal of Research in Music Education* 20, no. 4 (Winter 1972): 469-76.

> Shows diversity of attitudes about school music in the fifty years after the Revolutionary War.

B88. Gamble, Thomas. "The Father of American Church Music — Lowell Mason." *The Christian Observer*, June 25, 1919: 4-6.

> Occasion: the centenary of Bishop Heber's text for "Missionary Hymn." Cites a Lowell Mason manuscript in Henry Lowell Mason's possession, dating the tune as 1824 in Lowell Mason's hand. Recounts Mason's participation in Savannah's religious and musical life and the Goodrich connection leading to Mason's publishing with the Boston Handel and Haydn Society in 1821.

> Reports that the current Presbyterian hymnal contains 33 Mason tunes set to a greater number of texts. "Only one composer exceeds him in the number of tunes in that compilation and they are not used in anything like the degree that [his]...are." (6)

B89. -----. *Stories of Savannah*. Papers, manuscripts. Savannah Public Library, n.d.

> Collection of a dedicated amateur historian. Contains many documents relevant to Mason's years in Savannah.

B90. Gardiner, William. *The Music of Nature, or An Attempt to Prove That What is Passionate and Pleasing in the Art of Singing, Speaking, and Performing upon Musical Instruments, is Derived from the Sounds of the Animated World with Curious and Interesting Illustrations*. Boston: J.H. Wilkins and R.B. Carter, 1837. Originally published in England, 1832.

> Contains chapters on physical faculties, oratory and language, individual instruments, and vocal performance techniques. Argues that singing is conducive to good health. Given Mason's esteem for

Gardiner's work, this is a book he must have welcomed and absorbed.

B91. Gary, Charles L. "Vignettes of Music Education History." *Music Educators Journal* 48, no. 5 (April/May 1962): 56.

Easily accessible source with a photograph of Mason with William B. Bradbury and George F. Root. Includes anecdote by Frederick Root, son of George Frederick Root, with Mason's assertions that "older and more competent teachers...should be introducing the subject [music]. Therefore...I would start the new teachers in the upper grades and promote them down...as they ripened in service."

B92. Gellerman, Robert F. *The American Reed Organ: Its History; How It Works; How to Rebuild It.* New York: The Vestal Press, 1973.

Covers the history of Mason & Hamlin, including Lowell Mason's role in its founding. Abundant illustrations.

B93. "The Germania Musical Society." *Dwight's Journal of Music* 5, no. 24 (September 16, 1854): 189.

Quotes from the Newport *Daily News* concerning music libraries. Cites Lowell Mason's library as one of the four best music libraries in the country (three of the four owned by individuals and the fourth by the Harvard Music Association of Boston and Cambridge with its 300 to 400 volumes). Remarks that in public libraries of 80,000 to 100,000 volumes, scarcely 50 volumes of music literature can be found.

B94. Gilman, Samuel. *Memories of a New England Village Choir with Occasional Reflections by a Member.* Boston: S.G. Goodrich & Co., 1829.

Fascinating, firsthand account of choir problems typical in the early nineteenth century. Narrative style, based on the author's experiences. (cf., Hastings, *The History of Forty Choirs*, B113.)

B95. Gilmore, Patrick S. *History of the National Peace Jubilee and Great Musical Festival Held in Boston, June, 1869, to Commemorate the Restoration of Peace Throughout the Land.* Boston: P.S. Gilmore, 1871.

> Includes letter of invitation to Lowell Mason and his response. Mentions Henry Mason's $1000 contribution to the festival in the name of Mason & Hamlin.

B96. Gons, Marie Otken. "Survey of American Music Textbooks, 1830-1890." Master's thesis. Rutgers University, 1972. 118 pp., illustrations.

B97. Goodwin, Thomas. *Sketches and Impressions, Musical, Theatrical, and Social (1799-1885). Including a Sketch of the Philharmonic Society of New York.* New York: G.P. Putnam's Sons, The Knickerbocker Press, 1887.

> Useful study for finding parallels between music in New York and Boston during Mason's years, e.g., between the New York Philharmonic Society and the Boston Academy of Music orchestra in the 1840s. Anecdotal, autobiographical account. Goodwin (1799-1886) was a music librarian who emigrated to this country in 1827.

B98. Gould, Nathaniel D. *Church Music in America: Its History and Peculiarities at Different Periods, with Cursory Remarks on Its Legitimate Use and Its Abuse; with Notices of Schools, Composers, Teachers and Societies.* Boston: A.N. Johnson, 1853. Reprint. New York: AMS Press, 1972.

> "The principal design of the following pages is to give a plain, simple and concise account of Sacred Music in America for the last eighty years." (Introduction) The first two chapters ("Bible History of Music" and "Ancient Church Music in Europe and America") lead into discussion of psalmody and "progress" (with Law, Holyoke, Kimball, Shaw) and into the establishment of school music. Much vague discussion without ties to specific people or events. No index. The list of books of sacred music for schools and churches from 1810 on is of interest, though incomplete. Important as mid-century commentary by a practicing music teacher.

B99.   Graber, Kenneth G. "The Life and Works of William Mason (1829-1908)." Ph.D. diss., University of Iowa, 1976.

This study of Lowell Mason's pianist son includes a chapter about his early training and environment in Boston and his participation in conventions and institutes. The focus is William's musical training and accomplishments as a composer, performer, and piano pedagogue.

Indicates that Lowell Mason did not want William to pursue a music career, despite the boy's obvious talent and interest; rather, Williams' father wanted him to become a cleric. " William's early training [in music]...was entrusted entirely to his mother, fostered by the musical atmosphere which naturally prevailed in the home of a professional musician." (6) When, by the age of twenty, William was clearly destined to become a professional musician, "the primary concern of Lowell Mason...became that of providing his son with the best musical training available." (10)

B100.   Gray, Arlene E. "Lowell Mason's Contribution to American Church Music." M.M. thesis, Eastman School of Music, 1941.

Focuses on her analysis of twenty-five selected hymn tunes. Thorough, though limited in scope. Conclusions reinforce those of other researchers, such as Howell, B130.

B101. Gray, Mary Sturgis. "George James Webb: His Life and Compositions." Manuscript, Boston Public Library, 1937.

"In loving memory of my great uncle, George James Webb." Brief; family stories and pictures. Vague, no documentation but some information on Webb's family home in England and his life in Boston. Credits Webb with the first American use of a baton in conducting orchestras.

B102. Grimes, Calvin Bernard. "American Musical Periodicals, 1819-1952: Musical Theory and Musical Thought in the United States." Ph.D. diss., University of Iowa, 1974.

B103. Groves, Robert Westfall. "The Life and Works of W.S.B. Mathews (1837-1912)." Ph.D. diss., University of Iowa, 1981.

Survey's Mathews' life and his pedagogical concepts, examining 25 of his most significant books. Cites his pioneering in teacher certification and music organizations, such as MTNA. Appendices include lists of Mathews' piano works and all signed articles. For Mathews' connections with Mason, see B187-B191.

B104. Hadden, J. Cuthbert. "Lowell Mason, American Educator and Musical Pioneer." *Etude* 28 (March 1910): 165.

Brief summary originally printed in the English publication, *Musical Opinion*. Praises "this prince of early American psalmody reformers," sketches Mason's life, and offers anecdotes on the writing of some of his famous hymn tunes.

B105. ------. "Lowell Mason and Psalmody Reform." *The Choir Herald* 16 (November 1912): 21, 23.

B106. Hall, James William. "The Tune-Book in American Culture: 1800-1820." Ph.D. diss., University of Pennsylvania, 1967.

Examines two issues: (1) the roles the tunebook played in American culture of the early 19th century; (2) the relationship between these roles and the changing artistic values of Americans of the period. Describes tunebooks in general.

Hypothesis: New England tunebooks "took the lead in musical reform in the early nineteenth century, as native American musical compositions were rapidly replaced with those of English and Continental European composers. This reform in musical taste spread from New England, gradually diminishing in strength in more remote areas. In the western areas....the New England tunebook encountered strong resistance from...books which favored both folk hymn tunes and the compositions of older composers...." Analysis supports the hypothesis: the author found a strong correlation between standards of taste and geographic regions.

B107. Hamm, Charles. *Music in the New World.* New York: W.W. Norton and Company, 1983.

Offers "both a history of music in America and a history of American music." (xi) Good information on discography and other resources, plus an extensive bibliography arranged by topics. Provides the context of Mason's life and career.

B108. Harrington, Joseph Jr. "On the Practicability and Expediency of Introducing Vocal Music as a Branch of Education, into Our Common Schools." *The Lectures Delivered Before the American Institute of Instruction, at Lowell [Mass.], August, 1838.* n.p., n.d. Reprinted in B272, vol. 2, 220ff.

Harrington, principal at Hawes School during Mason's experimental year (1837-38), uses his observations of Mason's experiment in this defense of music in the schools.

B109. Harris, Ernest E. *Music Education: A Guide to Information Sources.* Detroit: Gale Research Company, 1978.

Well-organized, annotated source. Points to many topics related to Mason, including hymns and other religious music as well as music education. Covers histories of music education and studies of music education philosophies, facilitating the examination of Mason's work and philosophy in context. Includes source books, dissertations, and other useful materials.

B110. Harris, J. L. (Rev.) "An Hour with Dr. Lowell Mason." *The Christian Advocate.* 1871 or 1872 [?] (from a Henry Lowell Mason scrapbook in the MENC Historical Center.)

Reports visiting the eighty-year-old Mason and seeing his library. "Though somewhat feeble in body, he is cheerful, and his mind is apparently as vigorous as ever." In the library, saw a "huge folio as large as the largest family Bible. The print is very coarse, and the notes about an inch in length." This was Luther's hymn and tune book, meant to be set on a rack for a dozen or more singers to see. Also saw a copy of the Ainsworth Psalter. Says that Mason is preparing a treatise on harmony to be published within a year. A rare firsthand account concerning Mason's final months.

B111. Hartley, Kenneth R. *Bibliography of Theses and Dissertations in Sacred Music.* Detroit: Information Coordinators, Inc., 1966, 1967.

More than 1500 dissertations listed geographically and alphabetically. Author, composer, and subject indexes provided. Offers access to many studies related to aspects of sacred music during Mason's era.

B112. Hastings, Thomas. *Dissertation on Musical Taste: Or General Principles of Taste Applied to the Art of Music.* Albany: Websters & Skinners, 1822. New York: Mason Brothers, 1853. Reprint. New York: Johnson Press, 1968.

Deals with intonation, accent, articulation and other specifics of singing; qualities desired in church music, abuses in church music and proper management of choirs; the need to improve church music and means toward that end, including teaching children early. Basic to understanding Mason's concepts because Mason studied Hastings' ideas during his formative years in Savannah.

B113. -----. *The History of Forty Choirs.* New York: Mason Brothers, 1854.

Preface states that the incidents described are substantially true. "The leading object has been to afford useful instruction, in such manner as to avoid unpleasant personalities." Deals with such obstacles as clergy without musical taste, poor facilities, and lack of cooperation, plus other, more specific problems: e.g., patent notes favored by some, yet seen as an evil because they "hinder the people from acquiring any satisfactory amount of practical knowledge, and encourage low and limited views of the art." (154)

Parallels Mason's views and experiences, lends support to his work. Concerning "old tunes vs. new" and mal-adaptations (putting new sacred texts to popular secular music), the remedy fits Mason's practice: "Melodies which are new and attractive, and at the same time chaste and simple, are widely circulated in every direction. They have extensively taken the place of these mal-adaptations, and are supplying a want which has been deeply felt." (194)

B114. Heintze, James R. *American Music Studies: A Classified Bibliography of Master's Theses.* Detroit: Information Coordinators, 1984.

Information on each thesis: author, title, degree, discipline or subject other than music mentioned in the sources used, university, date completed, number of pages, illustrations, photos, plates. Topical arrangement; easy cross-checking with the index. Well-designed, excellent reference.

B115. Heliodore, Mary P. "Lowell Mason's Contributions to the Field of Music Education in America." Master's thesis. DePaul University, 1953. 54 pp.

B116. Heller, George N. *Historical Research in Music Education: A Bibliography.* Lawrence: The University of Kansas, 1986.

Bibliographical data on books, articles, masters theses and dissertations in music education, arranged by those categories. Useful for researching music education history before and during Mason's time. Offers detail on a wide range of twentieth-century materials, including the hard-to-find, unpublished works of graduate students.

B117. -----. "Review of *Lowell Mason: His Life and Work.*" *Music Educators Journal* 72 (December 1985): 59-61.

Provides a synopsis of Mason's career and reflects on his complexities as a person. "What emerges...is a portrait of a complex man of great and diverse talents pursuing deeply held principles in well-conceived and efficiently executed programs...a complicated human being who struggled with the world around him and with his own inner conflicts" and "whose influence on American music and music education was enormous." (60)

B118. Herz, Gerhard. *Bach Sources in America.* Ann Arbor, MI: UMI Research Press, 1984.

> Provides concrete detail about Bach works in the Lowell Mason Collection. Summarizes the Kittel/Rinck association and Mason's purchase of the Rinck library, holdings described as abounding in keyboard music "with organ compositions forming its solid core." (207)

B119. Higginson, J. Vincent. "Notes on Lowell Mason's Hymn Tunes." *The Hymn* 18, no. 2 (1967): 37-42.

> Focuses on twenty Mason hymn tunes based on Gregorian Psalm tones with music examples used to make comparisons. Illustrates the difficulty of tracing sources of Mason's tunes and of ascertaining where composing begins and arranging ends.

B120. Hillbrand, E.K. "How Music Found Its Way Into American Public Education." *The Etude* 42 (March 1924):163-64.

> Concise survey of contributions of Nägeli, Pestalozzi, Woodbridge, and Mason. Includes Horace Mann (1796-1859), Secretary of the Massachusetts State Board of Education during the time Mason was establishing music in the Boston schools. Stresses Mann's support for Mason's teaching. Mann's "Twelve Reports on the conditions of Education in Massachusetts, and elsewhere..." published passages supportive of school music. "It is important for us to see that a man was in office who knew the importance of what Mason was attempting to do." (163)

B121. Hinsdale, Burke A. *Horace Mann and the Common School Revival in the United States.* New York: Charles Scribner's Sons, 1898.

> Convenient, readable survey of the development of common schools before and during Mason's time and of Horace Mann's career. Chapters on Mann's unpopularity with Boston school officials aroused by his Seventh Annual Report (1843), comprising 188 pages in the five-volume *The Life and Works of Horace Mann* (Boston: Lee

& Shephard, 1891). Deals with the controversy over discipline, teaching methods, and teacher training generated by Mann's report; discusses the 154-page response published by 31 Boston schoolmasters in August 1844 and Mann's 176-page reply a few months later.

Mason began working with Mann the fall of 1845 in the Mann Institutes for Teachers. At the very same time (September 1845), Mason was dismissed by the Boston Public Schools, only to be partially reinstated, effective March 1846. Further work on Mason's career in the Boston Public Schools might well include a closer look at the Mason/Mann connection and the political climate surrounding Mann, Mason, and Boston school officials.

B122. Hitchcock, H. Wiley. *Music in the United States: A Historical Introduction.* 3rd ed. Englewood Cliffs: Prentice-Hall, Inc., 1988. (Annotations from the original edition, 1969.)

A compact history, including a brief, perceptive account of Mason's career. Describes Mason's hymn tunes: "based on European Classic-era music, [the style] is one of genteel correctness, neat and tidy in harmony and form, bland in rhythm and melodic thrust. The airs are now in the tenor voice, now in the treble; not infrequently, they are oddly awkward, perhaps because Mason's musical thought as a whole was dominated by considerations of harmony, and as a result even the air is sometimes made to accommodate the harmony rather than fulfilling its own directional impulse." (57)

Shows Mason as part of the "cultivated tradition" defined as "a body of music that America had to cultivate consciously, music faintly exotic, to be approached with some effort, and to be appreciated for its edification, its moral, spiritual or aesthetic values." (43) By contrast, music of the "vernacular tradition" is "more plebeian, native, not approached selfconsciously but simply grown into as one's vernacular tongue; music understood and appreciated simply for its utilitarian or entertainment value." (43-44)

B123. Hollander, Goldye. "The Life and Works of Dr. Lowell Mason, the Father of Public School Music." Master's thesis. Texas Agricultural and Mechanical College, 1941.

B124. Hood, George. *History of Music in New England with Biographical Sketches of Reformers and Psalmists*. Boston: Wilkins, Carter & Co., 1846. Reprint. New York: Johnson Reprint Corporation, 1970, with a new introduction by Johannes Riedel.

> Important because of Hood's vantage point. Adds relatively little about Mason himself but deals in some detail with his precursors. List of sacred works is valuable though incomplete. Includes letters from Mason, Webb, Nahum Mitchell, and A.N. Johnson, dated 1845, endorsing the book.

B125. Hooker, Edward W. *An Address Delivered Before the Hastings and Mason Musical Association at Pittsfield, December 25, 1837.* Pittsfield: Phineas Allen & Son, 1838.

B126. -----. *Music, as a Part of Female Education*. Boston: T.R. Marvin, 1843.

> Hooker, a Congregational minister in Bennington, VT around 1840, is one clergyman who took up the Boston Academy of Music's challenge to clergy and argued for music instruction in the public schools. Here he raises the common objections to music training for women: too expensive in time and money, considering that music will be set aside later for domestic duties; too much music accompanies "poetry of a light and frivolous character." (4)

> Refutes the objections with arguments used by pioneer music educators: music is God's gift to be cultivated gratefully. Deplores tasteless texts, their "absolute insipidity, with the declarations or sighing or groaning of love"; like "nine tenths of the novels of our day," such music belongs "in one vast pile, with torches applied on all sides of it." (13) Hooker's reasoning and arguments are not so gender specific as the title suggests.

B127. "Horace Mann." *The American Journal of Education* 5, no. 15 (December 1858): 611-56.

> Summary of Mann's career, including his twelve years as Secretary of the Massachusetts State Board of Education (1837-1848), the years

of Mason's work in the Boston Public Schools. Provides a synopsis of the twelve reports Mann issued, revealing his far-sightedness about public education. Lists his publications and prints a speech made at the dedication of the State Normal School-House at Bridgewater, 1846.

Reprints the "Memorial of the Directors of the American Institute of Instruction" drawn up by Boston educator George B. Emerson, appealing to the legislature in 1836, asking for the appointment of a state superintendent of the common schools. (653-56) Notes that "in every way in which it was claimed [by Emerson] an officer might act for the good of the schools, Mr. Mann did act with wonderful efficiency and the largest results." (640)

B128. Howard, John Tasker. *Our American Music.* Revised, 4th ed. New York: Thomas Y. Crowell & Co., 1965.

Concise, basic information about Mason and his contemporaries, providing perspective of the era. Excellent bibliography and index.

B129. Howard, John Tasker, and George Kent Bellows. *A Short History of Music in America.* New York: Thomas Y. Crowell, 1957.

Brief but clear summary of Mason's career with attention to Mason's part in bringing "My Country, 'tis of thee" to the American public. Positive assessment: "Mason was the first to preach music for the masses, and he was responsible for higher standards of choral singing in America. He bridged the work of the old-fashioned traveling singing-teacher and the modern music school. He was one of the most powerful and original personalities of the nineteenth century, and he did more, perhaps, than any other one man of his time to further the cause of American music." (96-97)

B130. Howell, Lillian Pope. "Lowell Mason, Composer of Hymn-Tunes." M.S.M. thesis, Southern Baptist Theological Seminary, 1948.

Analysis of sixty hymn tunes yielding data on Mason's rhythmic, melodic, and harmonic practices. Comparable to Arlene E. Gray's study, B100, in depth and in its conclusions.

B131. Hubbard, William Lines, ed. *The American History and Encyclopedia of Music*. Vol. *VIII: The History of American Music*. New York: Irving Squire Toledo, 1908. Reprint. New York: AMS Press, Inc., 1976.

See Damrosch (B59) on music in the public schools. Unsigned chapters on "Psalmody and Church Music" and "The Music Trades" (on instrument manufacturing) are also useful.

Detailed information on church music, singing schools, and Mason's contemporaries. Little documentation. Interesting as evidence of the interpretations of early 20th century writers.

B132. Institute for Studies in American Music. *American Music before 1865 in Print and on Records: A Biblio-Discography*. Preface by H. Wiley Hitchcock. Brooklyn, NY: I.S.A.M., 1976.

Convenient source for finding music of the Mason era and earlier. Includes music in performance editions, facsimile reprints and books, plus a discography and index to authors, compilers, and titles.

B133. Jackson, Richard, ed. *Democratic Souvenirs: An Historical Anthology of 19th-century American Music*. New York: C.F. Peters Corporation, 1988.

Contains a hymn tune by Mason ("Safely Thro' Another Week") as well as a biographical sketch and brief bibliography. (annotation by Don Gillespie of C.F. Peters, in a letter to the author, September 9, 1987)

B134. ------. *United States Music: Sources of Bibliography and Collective Biography*. Brooklyn, NY: Institute for Studies in American Music, 1973.

Annotated listing of reference works, historical studies, regional and topical studies, including church music. Useful directory for basic sources concerning Mason's era and fields of interest.

B135. Jenks, F.H. "Lowell Mason." *New England Magazine* 11 (January 1895): 651-67.

Informative, nicely illustrated article with much biographical detail. Summarizes church music in New England before Mason's era. Emphasis on Mason's contributions in church music, especially congregational singing.

B136. John, Robert W. "Elam Ives and the Pestalozzian Philosophy of Music Education." *Journal of Research in Music Education* 8, no. 1 (Spring 1960):45-50.

Discusses the Ives/Mason relationship and Ives' use of Pestalozzian methods before Mason.

B137. ------. "A History of School Vocal Instruction Books in the United States." Ed.D. diss., Indiana University, 1953.

Provides information on books prior to and contemporary with Mason's. Puts Mason's textbooks in perspective. Provides a basis for comparison between Mason's works and those of others; shows that Mason followed closely the trends of his times. (cf. B149)

B138. ------. "Nineteenth Century Graded Vocal Series." *Journal of Research in Music Education* 2, no. 2 (Fall 1954):103-18.

Describes the controversy between teaching via note reading vs. the rote-before-note approach advocated by Lowell Mason. Discusses texts by Joseph Bird, George B. Loomis and others, including Mason's *The Song Garden* (1864-1866), W106. Illustrated with pages from the books. Good documentation.

B139. ------. "Origins of the First Music Educators Convention." *Journal of Research in Music Education* 13, no. 4 (Winter 1965):207-19.

A "synoptic historical account of the 'mother' organization of American music conventions." Traces the first several years of the Mason meetings and accomplishments of each convention, 1834 through 1841. Tables list names of members during these years, plus 1845. Valuable information, based on primary sources; useful bibliography.

B140. ------. "The Second Hundred Years." *Music Educators Journal* 51, no. 4 (February/March 1965):103-4.

These "second hundred years" are marked from the Mason textbook series *The Song Garden* (1864-1866), W106, that "instituted the concept of a sequential set or series of related song books for American school children. To the long list of other 'firsts' credited to Lowell Mason, we...add this accomplishment." (103) The series was a model but didn't sweep the country because teachers were not ready for the concept and because the third book was "quite advanced" (too advanced for most schools of the day). *The Song Garden* sold more on Mason's name than on "pedagogical uniqueness."

B141. Johnson, Artemis N. "On Vocal Music in Common Schools." Lecture 8 in *The Lectures Delivered Before the American Institute of Instruction at Hartford, August, 1845, Including the Journal of Proceedings, and a List of the Officers.* Boston: William D. Ticknor & Co., 1846.

Argues for music in the schools, discusses rote singing and its place, saying he would like to see rote singing in the primary schools with formal music training in later school years. Summarizes the Boston Public School music program as it developed after 1837: students spend most of their time on learning the "rules and principles of music. In the limited time devoted to the music lesson [two half hours each week], there is not much opportunity for actual practice," but students find other opportunities to practice, some in church choirs.

"I am acquainted with several choirs in Boston, in which are scholars of the public schools, who, with no other knowledge of the principles of music than they have acquired in school, equal, and in not a few instances, excel the older members of the choirs." (262)

B142.   Johnson, H. Earle. "Early New England Periodicals Devoted to Music." *Musical Quarterly* 26 (1940): 153-61.

Convenient guide to periodicals contemporary with Mason's career, offering descriptive summaries of periodicals prior to *Dwight's Journal of Music*, the thirteenth music journal in New England up to 1852. All but one of those journals was issued in Boston; none of them survived a third year, leaving the field open to Dwight.

Covers the two-year life of Parker's *The Euterpeiad*, 1820-1822, where Mason's first book won acclaim. Also Mason and Webb's *The Musical Library* (1835), W26, and *The Boston Musical Gazette* (1838), edited by Bartholomew Brown (but influenced by Mason).

Discusses H.W. Day's *The Musical Visitor* (24 issues) and *Juvenile Minstral* [*sic*], both in 1840-41, and quotes Webb's denunciation of Day and his praise of H. Theodore Hach's *The Musical Magazine*, first issued on January 5, 1839. Others mentioned include A.N. and J. Johnson's *The Boston Musical Gazette*, 1846-1848. (cf. B77)

B143.   ------. *Hallelujah, Amen! The Story of the Handel and Haydn Society of Boston.* Boston: Bruce Humphries, 1965.

Information on the practice of music societies' involvement with book publishing generally and the publishing of this society specifically, including the Mason collection of 1822 (W2). Describes Mason's first meeting with George K. Jackson.

B144.   ------. *Musical Interludes in Boston 1795-1830.* New York: Columbia University Press, 1943.

Fine source of information; draws heavily on newspapers of the time. Extensive material on books, periodicals, musical leaders such as George K. Jackson. Rather general concerning Mason, but valuable for describing the Boston scene into which Mason moved in 1827.

B145.   ------. "Notes on Sources of Musical Americana." *Notes*, Series II. 5 (March 1948): 169-77.

Summarizes holdings of selected city libraries, private libraries, and state historical societies. Encourages researchers to seek materials in a wide range of sources.

B146. Johnson, James C. "The Introduction of the Study of Music into the Public Schools of Boston and of America." *The Bostonian* 1 (March 1895): 622-32.

Account by a Mason pupil and associate. Describes schoolhouses of Boston in Mason's day and Mason's teaching. (B210, 118-19.)

B147. Jones, F.O., ed. *A Handbook of American Music and Musicians: Containing Biographies of American Musicians and Histories of the Principal Musical Institutions, Firms and Societies.* Canaseraga, NY: F.O. Jones, 1886. Reprint. New York: Da Capo Press, 1971.

Alphabetically arranged sketches of people and organizations with concrete information on each. Provides data on Mason's lesser-known associates, such as B.F. Baker and G.W. Lucas. In error on Mason's *Musical Letters from Abroad*, B7; the work grew from the trip of 1852-53, not the trip of 1837. Overall useful source of information, much of which is not readily available elsewhere.

B148. Jones, Merilyn. "Lowell Mason's Contributions to American Music." *American Music Teacher* 27 (June/July 1978): 24-27.

Based on Chase (B47) and Birge (B30), a lecture summarizing Mason's career in education and church music. Condenses Mason's teaching techniques into specific points.

B149. Jones, Walter R. "An Analysis of Public School Music Textbooks Before 1900." Ed.D. diss., University of Pittsburgh, 1954.

Factual, statistical information about school texts, offering bases for comparison between Mason's textbooks and those of others. (cf. B137, B138, B140.)

B150. Keene, James A. *A History of Music Education in the United States.* Hanover, NH: University Press of New England, 1982.

> Places Lowell Mason's work as a music educator in historical context. Useful, concise background on the climate of the early 1800s (96-102). Reasoned judgments: "Mason was an extraordinary promoter. What he may have lacked in intellectuality and originality, he made up for in resourcefulness and perseverance." (113) Tackles the stickiest issues of Mason's career: plagiarism of the *Manual of the Boston Academy of Music*, W20, and his dismissal, then reinstatement in the Boston schools, 1845-46. Nicely illustrated and indexed, a useful book.

B151. Kinnear, William B. "Lowell Mason—Some Teaching Peculiarities." *Musical Courier* 103 (July 11, 1931): 6.

> Using the 1836 edition of the *Manual of the Boston Academy of Music*, W20, deals with Mason's terminology (e.g., "half note, quarter note," and so forth, instead of "minim, crochet," etc.) and his pedagogy (e.g., teaching the scale through the use of syllables, numerals, "la," and words).

B152. Klein, Sister Mary Justina. *The Contributions of Daniel Gregory Mason to American Music: A Dissertation.* Washington, D.C.: Catholic University of America Press, 1957.

> Concise source of information on genealogy, including charts of the Mason family tree. Composer Daniel Gregory Mason (1873-1953) was one of Lowell Mason's grandsons.

B153. Kouwenhoven, John Atlee. "Some Unfamiliar Aspects of Singing in New England, 1620-1810." *The New England Quarterly* 6 (September 1933): 567-88.

> Discusses change of attitudes toward texts (Psalms vs. psalms and hymns) and music in colonial America, the move toward fuguing tunes and away from them, and the early 19th century move toward

sentimentality. By then, "Calvinism ...had been tempered by a more liberal clergy, but its militant ghost still stalked abroad, haunting the minds of the people who were enjoying the unripe fruits of a new freedom. The people could sing and dance now, but unripe fruit is bitter, and they felt a bothersome obligation to sing songs that made them weep, or which at least encouraged 'the most rigid virtue.'" (587-88)

B154. Kraege, Elfrieda A. "The Early Organs of the Fifth Avenue Presbyterian Church." *The Tracker* 18, no. 2 (Winter 1974): 3-10.

Provides detail about the church where Mason worked briefly, beginning May 15, 1853, and the George Jardine organ, described by Mason as "the best instrument of its size and contents which I have ever known." (4)

B155. ------. "The Masons and the Beechers: Their Crusade for Congregational Singing in America." *The Tracker* 25, no. 1 (Autumn, 1980): 101-8.

Well-documented examination of the church music climate at the Fifth Avenue Presbyterian Church, New York City, before, during, and after Lowell Mason's work there. Gives some insight into Mason's relationships with the clergy with whom he worked, from Boston in 1827 to Andover Seminary and the Orange, New Jersey congregation he helped build during his retirement years, 1854-1872.

B156. Kroeger, Karl. "Review of *Lowell Mason: His Life and Work.*" *Notes* 43, no. 3 (March 1987): 558-59.

Assesses modern interpretations of Mason's career perceptively: "Everyone wants to make Mason into something he never pretended to be and condemn him for falling below *their* expectations." (558) Summarizes content and organization of the book, B210, noting its limited coverage of Mason's music.

B157. Krummel, D.W., et al. *Resources of American Music History: A Directory of Source Materials from Colonial Times to World War II.* Urbana: University of Illinois Press, 1981.

Summarizes holdings of public and private libraries in all fifty states and the District of Columbia. Index guides researchers to specific libraries with holdings. Listing of library directories and sources also valuable.

B158. Kushner, David Z. "The 'Masonic' Influence on 19th-Century American Musical Education." *Journal of Musicological Research* 4 (1983): 443-54.

Critical of using music to serve non-musical ends: specifically, religion and morality. "By jumping on the Pestalozzian bandwagon and preaching morality through music at the very outset of his career in the Boston school system, Lowell Mason opened a Pandora's box from which educators have yet to extricate themselves." (451)

B159. LaFar, Margaret Freeman. "Lowell Mason's Varied Activities in Savannah." *The Georgia Historical Quarterly* 28, no. 3 (September 1944): 113-37. Reprinted in *Music in Georgia*, edited by Frank W. Hoogerwerf. New York: Da Capo Press, 1984.

Thoroughly researched, documented essay on Mason's Savannah years. Based on periodical literature, church records of his Savannah years, and correspondence with Henry Lowell Mason.

B160.   Lahee, Henry C. *Annals of Music in America: A Chronological Record of Significant Musical Events, from 1640 to the Present Day, with Comments on the Various Periods into Which the Work is Divided.* Boston: Marshall Jones Co., 1922.

Lists events with specific dates, places, and principal participants, indicating historic events contemporary with Mason's career. Limited commentary, offering only a general view.

B161. ------. "A Century of Choral Singing in New England." *New England Magazine* 26 (March 1902): 102-17.

Detailed account of choral societies, singing schools and early music conventions with firsthand accounts by participants. Time frame: from c. 1770 (Billings) to 1870 (the Great Peace Jubilee). Useful, but contains inaccuracies concerning Mason's career.

B162. Lang, Paul Henry. *One Hundred Years of Music in America*. New York: G. Schirmer, 1961.

Contains two essays directly relevant to Mason: Allen P. Britton, "Music Education: An American Specialty," B38, and Robert M. Stevenson, "Church Music: A Century of Contrasts," B248.

B163. Lawrence, Clara E. "Early School Music Methods." *Music Educators Journal* 25 (December 1938): 20-22.

Compares methods of singing school masters, Lowell Mason, and Luther Whiting Mason, with emphasis on continuing use of rote singing as an introduction to music instruction.

B164. Lawrence, Sarah B. "The Great Peace Jubilee." *New England Magazine* 32 (1905): 161-72.

Describes the planning of this event and the event itself. Shows the esteem in which Lowell Mason was held by leading social and political figures of the day.

B165. Lebow, Marcia Wilson. "A Systematic Examination of the *Journal of Music and Art* Edited by John Sullivan Dwight: 1852-1881, Boston, Massachusetts." Ph.D. diss., University of California, Los Angeles, 1969.

Discusses Dwight's efforts to encourage music libraries (the Boston Public Library and Harvard University Library in particular) with mention of Dwight's esteem for Mason's private library. Assesses Dwight's importance as "more than the first serious music critic for the United States; he was a pioneer in its development as a musicological center. As historian, translator, editor, bibliophile, and patron in this field, he has made an obvious impact. His journal, in these respects, is a recorder of fact." (316)

B166. Lichtenwanger, William, ed. *Oscar Sonneck and American Music*. Urbana: The University of Illinois Press, 1983.

> Deals with European and American influences on American music with only brief, but perceptive references to Mason: "Ever since the middle of the eighteenth century, this country has been an El Dorado for European virtuosos, teachers, conductors, publishers, and others active in music. No doubt America owes a great part, probably the greater part, of her musical life to these influences. It would be narrow-minded and ridiculous to favor expulsion politics. Men like Theodore Thomas have done perhaps more for the cultivation of musical taste in this country than any individual Yankee, with the exception of Lowell Mason and a few others." (13-14)

B167. Loveland, Karl. "The Life of Charles Zeuner: Enigmatic German-American Composer and Organist (1795-1857)." *The Tracker* 30, no. 2 (1986): 19-28.

> Describes the musical scene in Boston during the 1830s and 1840s, particularly church music and concert work of the Handel and Haydn Society. As president of the society, Mason worked with Zeuner, the society organist. Suggests that it was Mason who persuaded the society to obtain a skilled organist (19); Mason may have been instrumental in getting Zeuner to emigrate to Boston, perhaps through Woodbridge. Describes the Boston Academy of Music's experience in producing Zeuner's oratorio. Excellent bibliography, list of Zeuner's works, illustrated.

B168. Lowens, Irving. *Music and Musicians in Early America*. New York: W.W. Norton & Co., 1964.

> Essays on music and musicians, some earlier than Mason and some contemporaneous, offering readable, well-documented information. Valuable background on attitudes and figures in Mason's era: e.g., J.S. Dwight, "virtually the Transcendental pope of music," and his concepts (Chapter 15); connections between democracy and music (Chapter 16); and American traditions in church music (Chapter 18).

B169. ------. "Our Neglected Musical Heritage." *The Hymn* 3 (April 1952): 51-52.

Provides a concise description of the pattern used by American tunebook compilers, including Mason.

B170. Lucas, George Washington. *Remarks on the Musical Convention in Boston.* Northampton, MA: the author, 1844.

Strident criticism of Mason and his handling of the conventions. Undocumented charges by a firsthand observer, but fascinating for insights into personalities. Lucas (b. 1800) was a pupil of Hastings; a lecturer on music and teacher of vocal music; a resident of Northampton, MA from 1820-35, of Charlestown, MA from 1835-37, and of Troy, NY from 1837-44. He was president of the National Musical Convention in 1843. His whereabouts after 1852 or 1853 were not known. (B147, 87)

B171. McCabe, Martha R. "Early American School Music Books." *School Life* 24, no. 10 (July 1939): 290-91, 319.

A quick view of Mason's juvenile books, plus those of his contemporaries, including quotes from some prefaces. Lists about twenty books with bibliographic data and indications of library sources for many of them.

B172. McConathy, Osbourne. "Evolution of Public School Music in the United States: Part I. From Lowell Mason to the Civil War—a Period of Pioneers." *MTNA Proceedings 1922,* Pittsburgh, PA: 158-66.

Short sketches of the careers of Lowell Mason and Luther Whiting Mason with more detail about the latter. Draws "the important distinction between the music teaching developed directly or indirectly by the Boston Academy of Music and the spirit which it represented, and the musicians and teachers who came from Europe....In the former the ideal was primarily the socializing of the group through music....In the latter, the individual was the one consideration and individual talent..., leading to the professional equipment of the student, was the single consideration." (165)

B173. McCusker, Honor Cecilia. *Fifty Years of Music in Boston: Based on Hitherto Unpublished Letters in the Boston Public Library.* Boston: Trustees of the Library, c. 1938. Printed in *More Books*, the Bulletin of the Library, October, November, December 1937.

Essays by an assistant in the rare book department of the Boston Public Library, based on about 200 letters to John Sullivan Dwight from musicians and companies.

Covers Dwight's part in establishing of the Harvard Musical Association in 1837. Shows that goals of that organization parallel the goals of pioneer music educators in 1837: "The ultimate object proposed is the advancement of the cause of music....We would see it professed, not by the killers of time only, and those who scrape the fiddle for bread, but by the serious promoters of the best interests of the young....We may aim to have regular instruction introduced in the College....We may collect a Library of Music and works relating to it...." (9-10)

Discusses American students in Germany, including William Mason in 1849, a pupil of Moscheles, later Liszt. Describes the musical training Americans got in Europe.

Gives insight into figures and organizations of the day, most related to Mason indirectly, as in the case of A.W. Thayer, whose weak health and frustration in trying for publication is vivid: "never robust, [he] broke down under the strain, and he was ransacked with headache if he used his eyes for more than a few hours a day." (18)

B174. MacDougall, Hamilton C. *Early New England Psalmody: An Historical Appreciation 1620-1820.* Brattleboro, VT: Stephen Daye Press, 1940.

Classifies Mason as part of the new era from c. 1820-1870, an era begun by publication of Mason's *Handel and Haydn Society Collection* (1822), W2. Accurate on Mason, but brief. Cites Binney's *Congregational Church Music* (1853), "interesting as introducing Lowell Mason in connection with English psalmody. 'His tunes had a long run of popularity, especially among Non-conformists and are not likely to be soon forgotten, if only modern editors will leave the original but effective harmonies alone.'" (149) That statement reflects the thinking of James T. Lightwood, *Hymn-Tunes and Their Story* (London, Charles H. Kelly, 1905), 294-95.

B175. McGuire, David C. *Mus-Ed-Graphs*. Denton, TX: by the author, 1985.

Five charts on the history of music education in the United States, showing people, ideas, events, and publications chronologically, juxtaposed against events in literature, politics, and education. Eye-appealing, practical aid in aligning other events in history with events in music education.

B176. Mark, Michael L. *Source Readings in Music Education History*. New York: G. Schirmer, 1982.

Includes an excerpt from Mason's *Manual of the Boston Academy of Music*, W20, giving reasons why vocal music should be cultivated. Fine reference work, offering carefully chosen passages from philosophers, theologians, and other writers. Facilitates the tracing of Mason's ideas and the comparing of his ideas with those of others.

B177. Marrocco, W. Thomas and Harold Gleason. *Music in America: An Anthology from the Landing of the Pilgrims to the Close of the Civil War, 1620-1865*. New York: W.W. Norton & Company, Inc., 1964.

"Mason and His Contemporaries," (Chapter Six), offers a quick, convenient look at representative compositions.

B178. Mason, Daniel Gregory. "A Glimpse of Lowell Mason from an Old Bundle of Letters." *The New Music Review and Church Music Review* 26, no. 302 (January 1927): 49-52.

Consists of letters to his son William Mason on April 12, 1855, and William's wife, Mary Isabelle (Webb) Mason on January 8, 1857. The letter to William conveys Lowell Mason's view of music and its values; to Mary, on his sixty-fifth birthday, he describes himself as "a fresh spirit, young, blooming, almost ready, I hope, for eternal spring." Both are typical of Lowell Mason letters to family members.

B179. ------. "How Young Lowell Mason Travelled to Savannah." *New England Magazine* 26 (April 1902): 236-40.

Consists of two letters between Mason and his family, dated 1812 and 1813, concerning Mason's move to Savannah (quoted in B210, 12-15). Little commentary by D.G. Mason other than remarks about his grandfather's love of paradoxical statements.

B180. ------. "Lowell Mason." *Music Educators National Conference Yearbook* (1937) Chicago: MENC, 352-53.

A tribute to the "combination of idealism and shrewd practical sense" of the writer's grandfather. Also speaks of his brother, Henry Lowell Mason, and his work on a biography (B184).

B181. ------. "Some Unpublished Journals of Dr. Lowell Mason." *The New Music Review and Church Music Review* 9 (November 1910): 577-81; 10 (December 1910): 16-18; 10 (January 1911): 62-67.

Quotes from Lowell Mason's travel diaries of 1837, three small manuscript books that he filled with observations of social, religious, and musical matters, addresses, his itinerary, descriptions of menus, and quotes from devotional books. "That the religious and musical instincts were in him equally strong, that they were inextricably intertwined, the quotations from the journal...will show." (577) Quotes passages from the visit to England in the first two articles of the series, and includes part of the visit to Germany in the last article, with observations of church music, organ works, and school music.

B182. Mason, Henry Lowell. *Hymn Tunes of Lowell Mason: A Bibliography.* Cambridge: The University Press, 1944. Reprint. New York: AMS Press, 1976.

Detailed research. Listing of tunes according to their origins; indicates the book in which each tune first appeared. Prefaced by a concise summary of Mason's work as a hymn-tune composer/arranger. Further research on the tunes is needed; this work serves as a point of reference.

B183. ------. *Lowell Mason: An Appreciation of His Life and Work*. New York: The Hymn Society of America, 1941.

Twelve-page essay summarizing Mason's life and work with emphasis on his impact on church music. Informative, balances fact and interpretation.

B184. ------. "Lowell Mason Biography." Manuscript, Beinecke Rare Book and Manuscript Library, Yale University, 1957.

The unfinished labor of nearly fifty years by Lowell Mason's grandson. Chronologically organized. Much detail, thorough documentation throughout. Relies on Lowell Mason's diaries, correspondence, and family records, plus many nineteenth-century and early twentieth-century sources. Uses correspondence between Henry and people who had known Lowell Mason. To an extent impossible to determine, uses Lowell Mason diaries that have subsequently been lost. Covers Lowell Mason's life to about 1851.

B185. Mason, William. *Memories of a Musical Life*. New York: Century Co., 1901.

William Mason (1829-1908), the third son of Lowell and Abigail Mason, was a concert pianist. Here he offers impressions of people and events of his own times, but disappoints Lowell Mason researchers in his scant coverage of family matters and his perfunctory handling of Lowell Mason's role in America's musical life.

B186. Mason, William Lyman. *A Record of the Descendants of Robert Mason of Roxbury, Massachusetts*. Milwaukee: Burdick, Armitage & Allan, 1891.

Detailed family history by a nephew of Lowell Mason. William L. Mason (b. 1847) was the youngest son of Timothy B. Mason (1801-1861), one of Lowell Mason's brothers. Based on research in the Library of Congress and New York libraries, the book begins with

Robert Mason, immigrant from England in 1630 and continues to 1891.

B187. Mathews, William Smythe Babcock, ed. *A Hundred Years of Music in America: An Account of Musical Effort in America During the Past Century, Including Popular Music and Singing Schools, Church Music, Musical Conventions and Festivals, Orchestral, Operatic and Oratorio Music; Improvements in Musical Instruments; Popular and Higher Musical Education; Creative Activity, and the Beginning of a National School of Musical Composition, with Historical and Biographical Sketches of Important Personalities.* Chicago: G.L. Howe, 1889.

> Chapters on many topics, as indicated by the subtitle. Useful biographical sketches. Sees American music improving through a more thorough, general music education for the masses, a view that underlies his glowing assessments of Lowell Mason, whose "sagacious mind recognized...the most direct route to the building up of a general musical cultivation...[was] the education of the youth of the land." (36, 38)

> Challenges Ritter's assessment of Mason (cf. B231). Praises Mason's books of psalmody as "the first works of their kind published in this country which were respectable from a musical standpoint."(42)

> Most valuable as a witness to Mason's teaching: "Mason was a natural teacher, full of tact, logical, handy with crayon at the blackboard and delightfully simple in his phraseology...." (44)

B188. ------. "Lowell Mason, American Congregational Musician." *Music* 4 (September 1893): 527-30.

> Exaggerated praise for Mason: e.g., There was "no American music worth speaking of before his career began." (528) Includes anecdotes about the writing of some hymn tunes.

B189. ------. "The Lowell Mason Centennial." *Music* 1 (February 1892): 400-408.

Praises Mason as the "greatest musical educator this country has yet seen whose work elevated music teaching into an estate of public esteem which it never occupied before his time." (400) Adds some personal insight into Mason: "He was a gentleman of the old school. His house was always kept with a certain air of ease. Wine was at dinner, and was offered to visitors, to the last. Everything was decorous, well bred, and with a certain air of the grand seignor, which very much became him." (408)

B190. ------. "Lowell Mason, a Father in American Music." *The Musician* 16, no. 11 (November 1911): 721-22.

Mathews (1837-1912) first saw Mason at a teachers' institute in 1852 when he was only fifteen, then got to know Mason better in later years. Relates anecdotes, including the one in which William Mason shows Hauptmann one of his father's books. (B210, 142) Praises Mason's career.

B191. ------. "Lowell Mason and the Higher Art of Music in America." *Music* 9 (February 1896): 378-88; 9 (April 1896): 577-91.

Personal, highly complimentary evaluation of Mason to the almost total exclusion of factual material.

B192. Metcalf, Frank Johnson. *American Psalmody or Titles of Books, Containing Tunes Printed in America from 1721 to 1820.* New York: Charles F. Heartman, 1917. Reprint. New York: Da Capo Press, 1968.

Reference work more useful for works of Mason's predecessors and early contemporaries than for his own works. Lists dates, editions, place of publication for books of sacred music from Tufts (1721) to c. 1820; also indicates where these works can be found in about twenty-five American libraries. Of Mason's works, only *The Boston Handel and Haydn Society Collection* (1822), W2, is included.

B193. ------. *American Writers and Compilers of Sacred Music.* New York: The Abingdon Press, 1925.

Organized chronologically from Tufts and Walter to the revivalists and composers of camp-meeting music in the 1870s. Identifies each composer with a brief biographical sketch and description of works, sometimes with a discussion of specific tunes and/or books.

B194. ------. "Lowell Mason." *The Choir Leader* 23 (March 1916): 29-30, 34.

B195. Moore, Douglas. "The Activities of Lowell Mason in Savannah, Georgia, 1813-1827." M.F.A. thesis, University of Georgia, 1967.

One of the best sources of information on the Savannah years. Concise, though detailed and well documented.

B196. Moore, John W. *Complete Encyclopedia of Music, Elementary, Technical, Historical, Biographical, Vocal, and Instrumental. To which is added an Appendix, Introducing Musical Events to 1876.* Boston: Oliver Ditson Company, 1880.

Includes European and American musicians. "Psalmody" article has short sketches of composers and editors, but only Billings, Heinrich, and Holyoke get articles of their own. Information on William Goodrich under "Organ Building." Yields hard-to-find information, especially in the appendix.

B197. Mowry, William A. "Reminiscences of Lowell Mason." *Education* 13 (February 1893): 335-38.

Firsthand observations of Mason's conduct of an institute class in 1850. Praises Mason: "...of all men whom I have known, none excelled in address, adroitness, tact and skill in presentation, Dr. Lowell Mason....He was a broad minded, hearty, cordial, appreciative soul, and withal a born teacher." (336, 338)

B198. "Musical Conventions." *Dwight's Journal of Music* 1, no. 9 (August 14, 1852): 149-50.

Reflects upon music education as a popular movement for the general public vs. music as an art cultivated by an aristocratic elite. Sees "both good and evil in these great organizations of singing masters" but "we are sure the good preponderates." (149) Anticipates that the conventions will increase desire for "the highest culture." (150)

B199. "Music in Schools." *The Common School Journal* 4, no. 17 (September 1, 1842): 257-60.

The Tenth Annual Report of the Boston Academy of Music had been read in July 1842 and printed by T.R. Marvin. The report credits the academy with instituting public school music. Admits that music instruction in schools is "imperfect and elementary, but yet, Mr. Mason says, 'In all the schools, pupils may be found who can read common, plain music, with ease and accuracy,' an extremely desirable degree of attainment." (257) Notes that only two half hours a week are given to music.

Concludes that music in the schools has lived up to expectations. The academy report was supported by 21 letters from Boston grammar school principals testifying in favor of music. Letters from principals of Mayhew, Winthrop, Bowdoin, and Eliot Schools are printed here. Some say they changed their minds about music in the schools after seeing the good results over three years.

B200. "National Musical Convention." *The Musical Reporter* 1, no. 6 (June 1841): 255-60.

Summarizes the conventions at the Boston Academy of Music from 1834 through 1840, with attendance figures and remarks on content and governance. Urges the prompt issuance of convention reports; suggest that the forthcoming meeting (August 1841) will be the most significant ever. (260)

B201. ------. *The Musical Reporter* 1, no. 8 (August 1841): 368-71.

Lists classes and their instructors for the conventions run by the Handel and Haydn Society and by the Boston Academy of Music.

Noting that "of all classes of people, musicians are the most irritable, and most disposed to be quarrelsome," the writer urges every member to attend with "the sole object of musical improvement in his mind..." (369) Does not deal with the reasons why two conventions were running in Boston that year.

B202. Nesnow, Adrienne. "Lowell Mason Papers." A register compiled under a grant from the National Endowment for the Humanities. New Haven: Yale University, 1982.

Convenient listing of Mason materials, divided into music, correspondence, programs, clippings, writings (diaries vs. other), biographical information (including Henry Lowell Mason's manuscript biography), memorabilia, and other material, including documents concerning William Mason. Each document is dated (if possible) and located according to box and folder numbers.

B203. Nye, Russel B. *The Cultural Life of the New Nation: 1776-1830.* New York: Harper & Row, 1960.

Readable, informative background for the early life and career of Lowell Mason. Illustrated. Extensive topical bibliography, partially annotated.

B204. Ogasapian, John H. "Lowell Mason as a Church Musician." *Journal of Church Music* 21 (September 1979): 6-10.

Summary of Mason's career and contributions to church music with emphasis on congregational singing and music for congregations. Includes Mason's brief tenure at Fifth Avenue Presbyterian Church in New York City. Well-researched and illustrated.

B205. ------. "Review of *Lowell Mason: His Life and Work.*" *Journal of Church Music* 28, no. 2 (February 1986): 28-29.

Notes that a definitive work on Mason was long overdue. Reflects on Mason's "odyssey in church music...from massive and loyal urban choirs...to the suppression of choral music...in favor of congregational singing: the direct outgrowth, if his letters from Europe during his trip of 1852-3 are an indication, of his experience with the massed singing there, especially in Germany." (29) Review refers to B210.

B206. O'Meara, Eva J. "The Lowell Mason Library of Music." *The Yale University Library Gazette* 40 (October 1965): 57-74.

Precise, authoritative essay by one who knew the Mason Library and its history thoroughly through her long career as Music Librarian at Yale University. The finest source of detail on this topic.

B207. ------. "The Lowell Mason Papers." *The Yale University Library Gazette* 45, no. 3 (January 1971): 123-26.

Authoritative statement on the materials given to the Yale Music Library by the heirs of Henry Lowell Mason. Reviews the Henry Lowell Mason manuscript biography; describes in general terms the approximately 350 letters (of which about a third are by Lowell Mason). Discusses the relationship between the Mason family and George Blagden Bacon, their friend, confident and clergyman in Orange, New Jersey during Mason's retirement years.

B208. Paige, Paul Eric. "Musical Organizations in Boston: 1830-1850." Ph.D. diss., Boston University, 1967.

Shows Mason's role as minor in stimulating performances except for the Boston Academy of Music and the Musical Education Society. Good summary of musical activities during that period.

B209. Pemberton, Carol A. "Critical Days for Music in American Schools: November 1-14, 1837 and August 14-28, 1838." *Journal of Research in Music Education*, forthcoming 1988.

Explains events leading to the Hawes School experimental year, the nature of the experiment, and the interactions between people and events during August 1838 leading to the historic resolution of August 28, 1838. Shows that getting music accepted into the Boston public schools depended on a precarious balance of people and events. Draws heavily on research into Mason's life (B210, B211) and into the Boston school system of the 1830s (B272).

B210. ------. *Lowell Mason: His Life and Work.* Ann Arbor, MI: UMI Research Press, 1985.

> Definitive biography, based upon the dissertation of the same name (B211). Beginning and ending chapters arranged chronologically; middle chapters arranged topically for discussion of music education, church music, music publications, composing and arranging, travels abroad, the Mason Library, family matters, and teachers' conventions and institutes. Appendices list events and publications. Extensive bibliography, thorough indexing. (cf. B117, B156, B205.)

B211. -------. "Lowell Mason: His Life and Work." Ph.D. diss., University of Minnesota, 1971.

> Draws on nineteenth-century sources, including Mason's diaries and letters, and upon other archival material, such as the manuscript biography of Henry Lowell Mason (B184). Contains much the same organization and content as the book published in 1985 (B210), plus Mason's last will and testament; family genealogy; documents of the Boston Academy of Music; the Davis Report to the Boston School Committee, August 24, 1837; "How Shall I Teach," by Mason; an advertisement for Mason's lectures in London, 1853; and a tribute to Mason published in *The New York Musical Gazette,* February, 1873.

B212. ------. "The *Manual of the Boston Academy of Music,* 1834: A Remarkable Book from a Remarkable Era." *The Bulletin of Historical Research in Music Education* 7, no. 2 (July 1986): 41-54.

> Describes the *Manual,* its sources, purposes, organization, and significance. Demonstrates Mason's presentation with sample passages that teach the major third. Quotations reveal the book's style as well as contents.

B213. ------. "The Past is Prelude." *Music Educators Journal* 73, no. 9 (May 1987): 37.

> Suggests that history offers useful perspectives, including the values pioneer music educators found in teaching music.

B214. ------. "Revisionist Historians: Writers Reflected in Their Writing." *Journal of Research in Music Education*, forthcoming 1988.

> Contrasts 19th and 20th century interpretations of Mason's ideas and practices. Cites specific examples of praise and criticism accorded Mason during his lifetime and in later generations.

B215. ------. "Singing Merrily, Merrily, Merrily: Songs for the Skeptics of 1838." *American Music*, forthcoming 1988.

> Describes the Hawes Grammar School demonstration concert of August 14, 1838, and the experimental year (1837-38) when these public school children studied music in their schools. Includes a summary of the rationale behind the venture and representative songs included in the concert.

B216. Perkins, Charles C. and J.S. Dwight. *History of the Handel and Haydn Society of Boston, Massachusetts. Vol. I. From the Foundation of the Society Through Its Seventy-Fifth Season 1815-1890.* Boston: Alfred Mudge & Sons, 1883, 1893.

> The best source of detailed information on Mason's association with the society, including details of book contracts and sales. Based on primary sources, the work summarizes the society season by season, giving information on concerts, financial status, officers, and other exact details. Also interprets information.
>
> Assesses Mason's predecessor as president, Amasa Winchester: "his musical shortcomings," his absorption in preparing and publishing sacred music, and his "countless acts of kindness." (94-95) Relates Mason's election of September 3, 1827, and says the society got "a very able teacher and a strict disciplinarian," (95) and a leader "not so very much superior to the members as to be unreasonably impatient at their shortcomings." (95-96)

B217. Perkins, H. Victor. "First Public School Music Teacher." *Music Educators Journal* 28 (September/October 1941): 12-14.

Summarizes Mason's life and contributions. Quotes from Beard's *The Rise of American Civilization* regarding Mason's broad interests and wide significance. Inset article by Frances E. Clark discusses the Mason sesquicentennial in 1942.

B218. Perrin, Phil D. "Pedagogical Philosophy, Methods, and Materials of American Tune Book Introductions: 1801-1860." *Journal of Research in Music Education* 18 (Spring 1970): 65-69.

Describes the pedagogical shift from pre-Mason to Mason's era and beyond: teaching the components of music reading separately vs. teaching them in combination. Focuses on the spread of principles called "Pestalozzian."

B219. Pierce, Edwin Hall. "The Rise and Fall of the 'Fugue-Tune' in America." *The Musical Quarterly* 16, no. 2 (April 1930): 214-28.

Defines fugue tunes, describes the environment in which they appeared, discusses Tufts, Walter, and Billings works with illustrations. Finds stylistic vestiges of fugue tunes in the works of Bradbury and Mason: "Occasionally...there are instances of 'points of imitation,' or of voices entering singly but without definite points of imitation, which show the influence of this older style. A favorite device is to have one phrase in a hymn-tune — usually the penultimate phrase — sung by a solo voice, or by *soli* duet, the concluding phrase to be sung *tutti*, in full harmony. Where any of these hymns have survived...modern editors have almost invariably altered them to simple four-part harmony." (224)

Shows samples of fugue tunes reprinted in books of the 1850s, but cites examples in books by Hastings and Woodbury, not Mason. Observes that this music often takes a "*macabre* outlook on life, both in words and in music," though Billings stands apart for "cheerful and manly sentiment...a praiseworthy tendency." (228)

B220. Place, Charles A. *The Early Forms of Worship in North America*. Worcester, MA: American Antiquarian Society, 1930.

Place, a Unitarian minister and author, sketches forms of worship to about 1825, dividing worship forms into liturgical, partially liturgical, and non-liturgical—the latter the most germaine to Mason. Uses primary sources, such as descriptions of services written by clergy in church records. Seeks to delineate order of worship, the amount and types of music, including the books used. Limited usefulness, brief but specific background information on practices of Mason's early years.

B221. Porter, Edith K. and Albert C. Ronander. *Guide to the Pilgrim Hymnal.* Philadelphia: United Church Press, 1966.

Represents hymnal companions, a source of data and anecdotes about the composing of hymn tunes. Some concise, detailed information, well-indexed; some material to be used with much caution, as here, attempts to trace bits of Handel's music in "Antioch," while recognizing Ebenezer Prout's opinion that the music is "very far from Handel." (107)

Mason himself is credited with this account: Parks and Phelps, his co-editors in several hymnal projects, had "applied to me for a musical setting for the hymn, 'Nearer, my God, to Thee.' The metre was irregular. But one night some time after, lying awake in the dark, eyes wide open, through the stillness of the house the melody came to me, and the next morning I wrote down the melody." (274)

B222. Porter, Ellen Jane Lorenz. "The Devil's Good Tunes: The Secular in Protestant Hymnody." *The Diapason* 63, no. 2 (January 1972):18-20.

Summarizes efforts to "bring the people to the hymns and the hymns to the people" through adaptations of secular music, including Mason's efforts. Summarizes sacred use of secular music from Luther's day forward, contrasting the practices of the Mason era: "Formerly, secular tunes had been introduced because the people knew them already and responded quickly to them. But the mid 19th-century introduction of secular classics as hymn tunes took place because a group of sophisticated musicians thought the people *ought* to know them, and also believed that their offering to God should be of the greatest music ever written." (20)

B223. ------. "A Hymn-Tune Detective Stalks Lowell Mason." *Journal of Church Music* 24 (November 1982): 7-11, 31-32.

Compares selected Mason hymn tunes with the sources from which they were arranged, showing that the arrangements vary from moderate to drastic alterations of the original.

B224. -----. "The Sunday School Movement." *The Hymn* 35, no. 4 (October 1984): 209-13.

Briefly surveys music books published for Sunday School use with some attention to Mason's books. Good discussion of texts considered appropriate for children during Mason's era. Suggested additional readings useful.

B225. "Public Singing in Schools." *The Common School Journal* 2, no. 6 (March 16, 1840): 82-83.

Notes that all over the state (Massachusetts) efforts are being made to introduce music into the schools. Reports on Col. Barr's "praiseworthy efforts to introduce singing" to about 150 school boys. (82) "The readiness with which they read the notes on the blackboard, give them the proper tones, and then transform them into some simple, but cheerful melody, cannot but gratify the dullest eye and please the most obtuse ear. The effect it has upon the taste, spirits, and manners of the boys, is surprising..." (82-83) (Barr was a Mason associate at the teachers' conventions: B210, 90.)

B226. "Reviews of Lowell Mason's *Musical Letters from Abroad.*" *Musical Opinion* 91 (March 1968): 327; *Pan Pipes* 6, no. 2 (1968): 49; *Response* 9, no. 2 (1967): 94-95; *Response* 9, no. 4 (1968): 184-85 (a reprint of the former).

Signed reviews. In *Pan Pipes*, a detailed, mostly objective summary of the book's contents. In *Response*, subjective observations, commenting, for instance, on the contradictions between Mason's "own poverty of inspiration" and his admiration for Bach and the Lutheran chorale. (95)

B227. Rice, Charles I. "Boston, the Cradle of Public-School Music in America." *NEA Journal of Proceedings and Addresses.* (1910): 798-803, and in *School Music* 11, no. 51 (September 1910): 36-40.

> Reports Boston in the 1830s had a population in the 60,000s, over 60 periodicals, 31 of them newspapers, 7 of those daily. (799) Relates events of 1836-37, quoting from the Davis committee report. Mentions the "evangelizing" of the Boston Academy of Music through its *Musical Tract No. 1*, containing the full Davis committee report and concluding, "May it [music] speedily be introduced as a branch of school instruction into every town and village in the land." (803)

B228. Rich, Arthur L. *Lowell Mason: "The Father of Singing Among the Children".* Chapel Hill: The University of North Carolina Press, 1946.

> Examines Mason's educational theories, tracing their origins, and comparing them with twentieth-century textbooks. Extensive bibliography; excellent, useful listing of Mason's publications and libraries in which they can be found.

B229. ------. "Lowell Mason, Modern Music Educator." *Music Educators Journal* 28 (January 1942): 22-24.

> Summarizes Mason's understanding of the learning process, his organization of material, and his division of singing classes into four main components: rote singing; song approach to note reading; note reading; part and choral singing.

B230. *The Rich Men of Massachusetts: Containing a Statement of the Reputed Wealth of About Two Thousand Persons, with Brief Sketches of Nearly Fifteen Hundred Characters.* 2nd ed. Boston: Redding & Co., 1852.

> Assesses wealth and provides brief but informative sketches, emphasizing how the wealth was attained and how much benevolence the individual showed. Statement on Lowell Mason published verbatim, B210, 136: $100,000 reputed wealth, equal to about $1,858,000 in 1986 purchasing power. (See note 37, p. 42.)

Reveals wealth of some of Mason's close associates, e.g., Samuel A. Eliot, from inheritance and marriage, 300,000; George B. Emerson, from marriage and his private school for wealthy young ladies, 100,000; Melvin Lord, bookseller, 150,000; John H. Wilkins, publisher, 100,000; Jonas Chickering, piano manufacturer, 300,000.

B231. Ritter, Frédéric Louis. *Music in America.* New York: Charles Scribner's Sons, 1883, 1890. New York: Johnson Reprint Corporation, 1970 (the 1890 edition).

Critical of Mason as a composer; rather, sees his "greatest merits...in his labors as a musical educator of children." (181) Recognizes the significance of the Mason Library and laments that it is not put to more use by theology students (176). Important as the view of a prominent interpreter of American music, though with obvious bias: opening with the "low state of musical culture" in the New World and seeing improvement in terms of European music and musicians' assuming larger roles in American culture. The summary of music in the public schools and in the churches (490-503) reflects what Ritter saw as a member of the generation immediately after Mason's life. (Ritter's dates: 1834-1891).

B232. Roorbach, Orville A. *Bibliotheca Americana: Catalogue of American Publications, Including Reprints and Original Works, from 1820 to 1861.* 4 vols. and supplements, "Together with a list of periodicals published in the United States." Roorbach, 1849; New York: G.P. Putnam, 1850; Roorbach, 1852; Roorbach, Jr., 1855; New York: Wiley & Halsted, 1858; Roorbach, 1861. Reprint. New York: Peter Smith, 1939.

Separate volumes but cumulative. From the card catalog at Widener Library, Harvard University about the 1852 publication: "Contains the whole of the original work published in 1849, the supplement published in 1850, also some two thousand titles of books then published and not contained in either...together with such publications as have appeared since...."

The work, continued by James Kelly (1829-1907), was published, then reprinted by Peter Smith under the title *The American*

Catalogue of Books, Original and Reprints, published in the United States from January 1861 to January 1866 with date of publication, size, place, and publisher's name.

B233. Root, George Frederick. *The Story of My Musical Life: An Autobiography.* Cincinnati: John Church Co., 1891.

Interesting reflections on Root's experiences with Mason and on the musical climate of his times. Frustrating in its lack of specificity and lack of documentation; casual, conversational tone.

B234. Ross, James H. "Lowell Mason, American Musician." *Education* 14 (March 1894): 411-16.

Anecdotes about the writing of some Mason hymn tunes. Compares popularity of his tunes with that of his contemporaries. Regards Mason as "the founder of national music" and "the father of a new church music," the latter as a promoter of congregational singing and "expressive tunes and singing natural and appropriate to the sentiments of the words." (412, 413)

B235. Routley, Erik. *The Music of Christian Hymnody: A Study of the Development of the Hymn Tune Since the Reformation, With Special Reference to English Protestantism.* London: Independent Press Limited, 1957.

Important book on hymnody with a brief but pointed summary of American hymnody, including that of the 19th century when American hymnody descended "into the slough of sentimentality" and "might have presented an unrelieved picture of music-hall sloppiness and camp-fire heartiness had it not been for the work of Lowell Mason." Mason is described as "a composer of indifferent merit...entirely defective in musical imagination," yet when set against his contemporaries, tunes like "Missionary Hymn" and "Olivet" are models of austerity and restraint. In essence, Mason's music is "often supremely dull, but he is very rarely vulgar." (166)

B236. Ryan, Thomas. *Recollections of an Old Musician.* New York: E.P. Dutton & Company, 1899.

Clarinetist/violinist Ryan, a member of the Mendelssohn Quintette Club, Boston, performed at many churches, theaters, and the Handel and Haydn Society from 1845 on. (For a summary of the club's western tours, see B173, 13-15.) Firsthand accounts of Webb's rehearsing the academy orchestra in a hopeless attempt at Mendelssohn's *Midsummer Night's Dream*. (46-47)

Lowell Mason "was never absent from any of our chamber concerts except when out of town. I well remember how, one night in the old Masonic Temple, when we had finished playing Mendelssohn's Quartette in D, op. 44, Mr. Mason rose from his seat in the second row, came to the stage, laid the score of the quartette at my feet, said, 'It was beautifully played; please keep the score; sorry I cannot stay longer,' and walked out in the stately, self-possessed manner so perfectly in keeping with his character." (115)

B237. Sabin, Robert. "Early American Composers and Critics." *Musical Quarterly* 24 (April 1938): 210-18.

Sees the American musical climate of the early 1800s as "crude, uninformed, inexperienced...but full of energy and new ideas." (210) Describes the American public of the day as "eager, ignorant, and conservative at heart." (213) Hastings' *Dissertation* (1822), B112, and *The Musical Magazine* (1830s) viewed in this atmosphere.

B238. Scanlon, Mary B. "Dr. Lowell Mason in Music Education." M.A. thesis, Eastman School of Music, 1940.

Thorough study with a sound discussion of Mason's work in music education. Good bibliography and illustrations.

B239. ------. Lowell Mason's Philosophy of Music Education. *Music Educators Journal* 28 (January 1942): 24-25, 70.

Contains Mason's detailed letter to his son William on April 12, 1855, a letter expressing his thinking about music and music teaching. Concludes that Mason's goal as a music educator was "subjective development, not objective attainment." (70)

B240. Schultz, Stanley K. *The Culture Factory: Boston Public Schools, 1789-1860.* New York: Oxford University Press, 1973.

Thorough, well-documented study. Offers insight into the community and school system where Mason worked to establish curricular music in the 1830s.

B241. Seaton, S.W. "Musical Instruction of the Young." *The Mother's Assistant* 2, no. 1 (January 1842): 10-11.

"I believe the time is already come, that in American schools, music is to take the place nature has assigned it...subserving the most valuable purpose in government and discipline of schools, in the education of the passions, by one of the most efficient means of moral training." (10) Endorses juvenile songs about nature, "each adapted to convey some pointed moral....songs reproving every evil passion....songs of reproof, of counsel, and instruction, with grateful hymns of praise and adoration." (11) A child's song by Lowell Mason is on the next page: "'I Can't' and 'I'll Try.'"

This monthly magazine, edited by William C. Brown, was published in Boston, primarily for women readers. This particular issue is part of the MENC Historical Center Collection, a gift of Henry Lowell Mason, evidently from Lowell Mason's personal effects.

B242. Seward, Theodore F. *The Educational Work of Dr. Lowell Mason.* n.p., 1879.

Twenty-one page commentary, praising Mason's work. Attempts to place Mason in perspective but is overly critical of his predecessors and of American music during the early 1800s. Evaluation reflects both Seward's era and his personal regard for Mason, though he did not always agree with Mason. Abigail Mason wrote that this essay "gives the best representation of my husband's work, and the only one of any value to the world." (B193, 217)

B243. Silantien, John J. "William Channing Woodbridge: His Life and Contributions to American Music Education." Master's thesis, Catholic University of America, 1972.

B244. Silver, Edgar O. "The Growth of Music Among the People." *NEA Journal of Proceedings and Addresses*. New York: The National Education Association, 1891: 813-20.

> Reports that a movement favoring music is well underway in America, partly through greater activity in the profession and partly through music in the schools. In reference to the latter, gives credit to the work of Woodbridge and Mason.

> Refers to a special report submitted two years before, based on 621 cities and towns in 1889, towns of 4,000 or more people. In 338, music was systematically taught in the public schools, and school officials viewed it favorably. Concludes that music in the schools has stood the "crucial test of experience and critical observation" (815) and that music should be taught not for its own sake alone, but for its positive effects on schools and pupils.

> Interesting as a study of parallels from one generation to another. This author echoes the arguments made for music in the 1830s: the human capacity is great and universal; music has social, intellectual, and physical advantages; and "the value of music as a unifying and humanizing force might well be the basis of the strongest plea that need be made for its universal recognition and encouragement, and especially for giving it a place in the education of the young." (818)

B245. "Singing in Common Schools." *The Common School Journal* 3, no. 12 (June 15, 1841): 189-90.

> Reports on advantages of having singing in the Boston Public Schools. Says it improves reading through practice with modulation (of vowel sounds) and articulation (of consonants). Also offers "a recreation, yet not a dissipation of the mind; a respite, yet not a relaxation." (190) States that discipline has not been impaired; rather, music has united the students with its kindly and pleasant influence.

> States that about 3,000 Boston school pupils now get music instruction. Quotes Mason, saying he's fully satisfied that "all may make some progress" because music is "a universal gift of Providence." (190)

B246.   Smith, F.S. "Recollections of Lowell Mason." *New England Magazine*, 11 (January 1895), 648-51.

> Valuable account by one who knew Mason well. Highly complimentary to Mason. Some factual data included; illustrated.

B247.   Stegall, Joel R. "Shape Notes and Choral Singing: Did We Throw Out the Baby with the Bath Water?" *Choral Journal* 19, no. 2 (October 1978): 5-10.

> Describes the shape-note movement and Mason's opposition, while noting Timothy and Lowell Masons' publishing of a shape-note book (W21). Shows that "social biases and inflexible thinking" can interfere with workable teaching devices. (10)

B248.   Stevenson, Robert M. "Church Music: A Century of Contrasts," in Paul Henry Lang, ed. *One Hundred Years of Music in America* (B162).

> Compares volume and popularity of Mason's works with that of his contemporaries. Mason "was so well able to gauge middle-of-the-road American musical taste that many of his hymn tunes were on the lips of the common folk within five years of their first publication. *Nearer, My God to Thee*, for instance, was considered within two years of publication to be one of the thirty most popular hymn tunes by the American Tract Society...that sponsored publication of the first Civil War hymnal for soldiers and sailors" (published in Boston, 1861). (83-84)

B249.   ------. *Protestant Church Music in America: A Short Survey of Men and Movements from 1564 to the Present*. New York: W.W. Norton, 1966.

> Chapter 8 offers detailed information on Mason and his contemporaries: their books, hymn tunes, sources, and musical styles. Richly detailed, yet concise documentation; useful bibliography.

B250. Stone, James H. "Mid-Nineteenth-Century American Beliefs in the Social Values of Music." *Musical Quarterly* 43 (1957):38-49.

> Summarizes the arguments made in favor of music in the schools. Shows that the arguments' appeal "was...strengthened by their association with contemporary viewpoints about education, human nature, and society." Schools fostered such ends as social progress, "Christian and practical ethics," and patriotism. (41) Cites 19th century authors and periodicals for support of views toward the arts. "In a society to which attitudes of philistinism were often ascribed, it is interesting to note the early development of public music instruction and the long-lasting ambitions of many American families to provide music education for their young people." (48) Shows convincingly that Mason was a man of his times in what he thought and promoted.

B251. Stopp, Jacklin Bolton. "A.N. Johnson, Out of Oblivion." *American Music* 3, no. 2 (1985): 152-70.

> Summarizes the career and contributions of Johnson, "a student, colleague and finally an antagonist to Lowell Mason." (152) Carefully researched and documented. Offers material not easily accessible about the Mason/Johnson era.

B252. Studwell, William E. "Lowell Mason: The Modest Music Maker." *The American Organist* 20, no. 7 (July 1986): 84-85.

> Suggests that Mason's reputation as a hymn tune writer would be enhanced were his actual output known. The tunes "Antioch" and "Hamburg" used as examples in which Mason was likely the composer, not just the arranger as he himself indicated in his books.

B253. Sunderman, Lloyd Frederick. "Boston and the Magna Charta of American Music Education." *Education* 69 (March 1949): 425-37.

> Stresses the importance of Boston in the rise of music education in America. Deals with objectives and achievements of the Boston Academy of Music in music teaching within the community. Summarizes events of 1836-38 in getting music into the school curriculum

and reports on growth and achievements in the early decades after 1838.

B254. ------. "Early Music Education in Massachusetts." *Education* 72 (September 1951): 45-67.

Summarizes the singing-school movement from about 1720 forward, the work of Woodbridge, Ives, and Mason around 1830, efforts leading to public school music in Boston, reports on Mason's work in Boston grammar schools after 1838, developments in school music elsewhere in the state, and music in primary schools (developed from about 1840-1864).

B255. ------. "The Era of Beginnings in American Music Education (1830-1840)." *Journal of Research in Music Education* 4, no. 1 (Spring 1956):33-39.

Discusses development of public school music in New York, Ohio, and Pennsylvania, paralleling developments in Massachusetts. Shows the influence of music academies and institutes.

B256. ------. *Historical Foundations of Music Education in the United States.* Metuchen, NJ: The Scarecrow Press, Inc., 1971.

Presents a summary of Pestalozzi's work and concepts, cites Horace Mann's leadership, and describes Mason's career. Sees Mason's "real significance" in the fact "that he was the first official supervisor of vocal music in the public schools of Boston." (46) Selective bibliography.

B257. ------. "History of Public School Music in the United States, 1830-1890." Ph.D. diss., University of Minnesota, 1939.

Summarizes the context of Mason's pioneer work: Chapter II, "Some Early Concepts of the Values of Music Education"; III, "The First Champion of American Public School Music" (Woodbridge); and V, "The Era of Beginnings, 1830-1840." Extensive bibliography. Includes tables, statistical information hard to obtain elsewhere.

B258. ------. "Sign Posts in the History of American Music Education." *Education* 62, no. 9 (May 1942): 515-50.

Presents material in five parts: (1) the era before public school music; (2) pioneer school music experiments; (3) Boston, the hub of American music education; (4) music in higher education prior to 1895; (5) some nineteenth-century interpreters of American music education. Concise; summaries in each of the five sections.

B259. Swan, John C., ed. *Music in Boston: Readings from the First Three Centuries.* Boston: Trustees of the Public Library of Boston, 1977.

Anthology of selections from the *Bay Psalm Book* (1640) to writings of music critic Henry Taylor Parker (1922). Excerpts from John Rowe Parker's journal *The Euterpeiad*, 1820-1822, include discussion of *The Boston Handel and Haydn Society Collection* (1822), W2, and a letter to the editor about that work. Reprints Chapter 1 of Mason's *Manual of the Boston Academy of Music* (1834), W20, and some of J.S. Dwight's writings on concerts of 1840-1841.

B260. Taylor, Millicent. "He Made America Sing." *The Christian Science Monitor.* January 3, 1942: 6, 12.

Summary of Mason's career with emphasis on his leading others to music, "as if wherever he lived and worked he could not help leading choirs, serving as organist in a church or two, and encouraging group singing." (6) This article was part of the sesquicentennial of Mason's birth, celebrated by the Hymn Society of America, MENC, and the Commission on Worship of the Federated Council of Churches of Christ of America.

B261. Tellstrom, A. Theodore. *Music in American Education: Past and Present.* New York: Holt, Rinehart and Winston, 1971.

Organized in five sections, beginning with Humanism and the Enlightenment, including the beginning of music education in the United States and Lowell Mason's Boston experience. Other sections: Industrial Age (the age of utility); Seeds of Progressivism; A

Period of Protest and Reaction (music education and determinism): and The Age of Experience and Experiment.

Purpose of the book: to gain "an ability of recognize the place of innovation." Each of the five sections opens with a chapter on the evolution and establishment of a major educational movement. Then the chapters demonstrate how the principles involved were transposed into action in the area of music education. (viii)

Summarizes the psychology underlying Mason's teaching, including the child's progressing at his own rate, learning as a result of interaction of the child with his environment, and learning by doing: "The child was rarely *told*, but rather was made to experience first those things about which he might learn. Learning was not a process wherein precepts were poured into the mind from the outside, but rather one of discovery on the part of the learner through his own efforts." (44)

B262. Thayer, A.W. "Lowell Mason." *Dwight's Journal of Music* **39 (November 22, 1879): 186-87; 39 (December 6, 1879): 195-96.**

Eloquent biographical summary and tribute by a former associate, one who "freely confesses that he had differed from Mr. Mason on various matters of opinion and taste; but this confession can only add emphasis to the expression of his deep appreciation of his many great qualities." (196)

B263. Thompson, James William. "Music and Musical Activities in New England, 1800-1838." Ph.D. diss., George Peabody College for Teachers, 1962.

Covers sacred and secular music, music societies, music publications, music journalism, and singing schools with many details difficult to find elsewhere. Excellent study; shows acceptance of school music as part of general cultural trends.

B264. Tilden, W.S. "Early Life of Lowell Mason: Address of William S. Tilden, President of the Medfield Historical Society, at Chenery Hall, Medfield, Friday, January 8, 1892, the Centen-

nial Anniversary of the Birth of Dr. Lowell Mason" in William Mason's autobiography, B185, 275-90.

> One of the best sources of information about Mason's early years. Some genealogical detail and anecdotes of the Medfield years.

B265. Trotter, James M. *Music and Some Highly Musical People.* Boston: Lee & Shepherd, 1878. Reprint. New York: Johnson Reprint, 1968.

> Biographical sketch of black musician Henry F. Williams with comments on Mason's association with him. Regrets that Mason, "who was so original and bold in music," did not throw his "great influence on the side of what he confessed was right," namely, equal opportunity for all Americans. (111)

B266. Upton, George P. *Musical Memories: My Recollections of Celebrities of the Half Century: 1850-1900.* Chicago: A.C. McClurg & Co., 1908.

> Reflects on some of Mason's contemporaries, such as G.F. Root, more than on Mason. Gives a view of American music after much of Mason's career, though with little connection between the musical climate and Mason's contributions.

B267. Van Camp, Leonard. "Choral Balance and the Alto Part in Early American Choral Music." *Choral Journal* 15, no. 9 (May 1975): 7-9.

> Choral practices from c. 1760-1800 with specific information about roles of the tenor and other voice parts. Valuable for authentic interpretations of music of that era and for understanding the practices of Mason's early years. (cf. B29)

B268. Wayland, Francis. "Introductory Discourse" by Francis Wayland, President of Brown University, at the First Annual Meeting of the American Institute of Instruction (March 1830). *The Schoolmaster: Essays on Practical Education Selected from the Works of Ascham, Milton, Locke, and Butler*; from *The*

Quarterly Journal of Education; and from *Lectures Delivered Before the American Institute of Instruction*. 2 vol. London: Charles Knight, 1836.

> Wayland and Mason were friends for many years, starting at least with the early years of the American Institute of Instruction. Wayland's thinking on education either helped shape Mason's, or Wayland and Mason reinforced one another's views. Here Wayland states his topic as "the object of intellectual education; and the manner in which that object is to be attained." (181)

> Suggests principles common to all teaching: (1) "Let a pupil understand everything that it is designed to teach him...by simplification and patience. Let a teacher first understand a subject himself. Let him know that he understands it. Let him reduce it to its natural divisions and its simplest elements. And then, let him see that his pupils understand it." (197)

> (2) Use frequent repetition. (197) (3) Practice. "Whether in arithmetic or grammar or logic, let exercise be so devised as to make the pupil familiar with its application. Let him construct exercises himself. Let him not leave them until he feels that he understands both the law and its application, and is able to make use of it freely and without assistance. The mind will never derive power in any other way. Not will it, in any other way, attain to the dignity of certain, and practical, and available science." (198)

B269. Wilhoit, Mel R. "The Music of Urban Revivalism." *The Hymn* 35, no. 4 (1984): 219-23.

> Discusses Joshua Leavitt's *The Christian Lyre* (1831) and the Mason/Hastings' response, *Spiritual Songs for Social Worship* (1832), W15, in the context of revival music of the nineteenth century. Discursive endnotes add useful information and references.

B270. Willis, Richard Storrs. *Our Church Music: A Book for Pastors and People*. New York: Dana and Company, 1856.

> General observations, helpful only as insight into thoughts of a Mason associate during his post-Boston years. Most revealing is

Chapter XII on "Mutilation of Hymns" by two practices: (1) "by solos, duets, etc. in the middle of a stanza"; (2) "by *invariable* interludes between the stanzas themselves." (108)   On interludes: "very few organists" do extempore playing well. (111)

Echoes Mason's utilitarian view of church music: "We have made, throughout, in these articles, a distinction between impressive and devotional music. In the first style...the words may be subordinated to the music: therefore interludes are here in place: the *general musical effect* being all that is cared for. In the second style, the music must necessarily be *subordinated to the words*: these words being addressed more or less directly to the Supreme Being—where any formal interruption of the sense and the continuous flow of the thought is not only improper, but, to my own mind, irreverent." (111-12)

B271. ------. "Reply to 'Attack upon Mr. Lowell Mason.'" *The Musical World and New York Musical Times* 5, no. 5 (January 29, 1853): 65-66.

Responds to criticism of Mason's use of the movable "do" and his composing of nothing more than Psalm tunes. Tries to put Mason's career in perspective: as a "practical musician" whose books fill "the popular want and the popular capacity" and are therefore "practicable...useful." (66)

B272. Wilson, Bruce Dunbar. "A Documentary History of Music in the Public Schools of the City of Boston, 1830-1850." Ph.D. diss., University of Michigan, 1973.

Comprehensive examination of the topic with a wealth of documents and clearly written, pertinent commentary. Presented in two volumes, the first consisting of major sections on events leading to curricular music in the Boston schools and on Mason's role before, during, and after 1837-38. The second volume presents verbatim documents from the Boston Academy of Music, the Boston School Committee, contemporary newspapers, and other relevant sources.

Indispensable for researching the climate in which public school music won formal acceptance and for understanding Mason's part in events. Also provides insight into Mason contemporaries and associates and on the teaching environment in Boston at the time.

B273. Wingard, Alan B. "The Life and Works of William Batchelder Bradbury, 1816-1868." D.M.A. diss. The Southern Baptist Theological Seminary, 1973.

> Traces and evaluates Bradbury's teaching, church work, piano manufacturing, and composing. Includes a catalog of 71 music books and an index of 1148 hymn tunes. Bradbury studied with Mason; Mason got him his first job. Includes analysis of Bradbury tunes with musical examples, illustrating eight types identified by the author.

B274. Winsor, Justin, ed. *The Memorial History of Boston, Including Suffolk County, Massachusetts, 1630-1880.* 4 vols. Boston: Ticknor & Co., 1880-1881.

> Contains a great deal of pertinent information on Boston during Mason's time. Illustrated, with plates, portraits, maps, plans, facsimiles. Includes such relevant essays are these: "Music in Boston" by J.S. Dwight; "Education, Past and Present" by Charles K. Dillaway; "The Fine Arts in Boston" by Arthur Dexter. (Justin Winsor was a librarian at Harvard.)

B275. Wolfe, Richard J. *Early American Music Engraving and Printing: A History of Music Publishing in America from 1787 to 1825 with Commentary on Earlier and Later Practices.* Urbana: The University of Illinois Press, 1980.

> Covers the development of printing methods, engraving and punching tools, ink and paper. Well-documented, with illustrations. Among the portions germaine to a study of Mason is Chapter X, "Customs and Conditions of the Trade," including a summary of copyright statutes in the U.S.A. starting with the first applicable law (Connecticut, 1781).

> Highly pertinent to Mason: describes consequences of the Copyright Act of 1790, a part of which read, "nothing in this act shall be construed to extend to prohibit the importation or vending, reprinting or publishing within the United States, of any map, chart, book or books, written, printed or published by any persons not a citizen of the United States, in foreign parts or places without the jurisdiction

of the United States." (192-93) The author's further comment: "Congress opened the door and even encouraged the pirating or reprinting of foreign music publications."

B276. Woodbridge, William C. "Music, as a Branch of Instruction in Common Schools." *American Journal of Education* 1, no. 7 (September 1830): 417-20.

Says vocal music is an essential part of school instruction in Germany and quotes an ordinance from a Prussian newspaper, January 15, 1828, to support his contention. The ordinance says that every teacher has a duty to teach singing and that pupils must be required to attend regularly.

Two things are needed for a similar course in this country: "a set of tunes adapted to the capacities of children, and calculated to associate the sensible with the moral and spiritual world in their minds, and *a simple analytical course of instruction*." Adds that Lowell Mason will soon be issuing a work to supply these needs, identifying it as *The Infant and Juvenile Lyre* [perhaps Mason and Ives' *The Juvenile Lyre*, 1831, W10]. That work "will be speedily followed by a manual for teaching, on a new and improved plan." (418)

Mentions a demonstration concert with a children's choir. Includes scores of two songs deemed appropriate for children's use: "The Morning Call" and "The Rising Sun."

B277. ------. "On Vocal Music as a Branch of Common Education." *The Introductory Discourse and Lectures Delivered in Boston, Before the Convention of Teachers, and Other Friends of Education, Assembled to Form the American Institute of Instruction. August 1830.* Boston: Hilliard, Gray, Little & Wilkins, 1831. Reprinted in *American Annals of Education and Instruction* 3 (May 1833): 193-212 (a journal owned and edited by Woodbridge) and in B272, vol. 2: 4-26 (the source to which page references below apply).

Describes his observations in Europe and his bringing back of materials for American use in hopes of getting appropriate music and methods ready for American school children. But another objective remains: "to awaken public interest, and inspire public confidence in music, probably the most difficult task." (5)

Presents arguments in favor of music teaching: to cultivate a God-given faculty and to use that faculty "to unite with our fellow Christians in expressing our gratitude and love to our heavenly Father." (9) Speaks of the physical and social advantages of music, then stresses its character-building potential, citing Plato as one source of support and noting the impact of well-chosen texts.

Uses observations of Pestalozzi and his followers to support the idea that all children can be taught to sing, with few exceptions; then cites the recent experiment in Hartford. Sets forth the principles of the Pestalozzian or inductive method as he interprets them to be.

B278. Wunderlich, Charles Edward. "A History and Bibliography of Early American Music Periodicals, 1782-1852." Ph.D. diss., University of Michigan, 1962.

Six chapters of summary and discussion plus an extensive "Chronological and Descriptive Bibliography of Early American Music Periodicals, 1782-1852." Contains detailed information on time, place, and length of publication, changes in titles, subscription prices, editors and important contributors, topics of articles published, listings of music contained in each issue, and location in selected libraries. Includes 783 pages, illustrations. Valuable reference work with much hard-to-obtain information, plus interpretations.

B279. Zinar, Ruth. "Music Education in Early America." *The American Music Teacher* 28, 1 (1978): 24, 26.

Shows connections between singing in church, singing schools, and public schools. Offers an overview of academies and monitorial schools.

Classified Listing of Works

The list below is a slight modification of material previously published in *Lowell Mason: His Life and Work*, ©1985, 1971 by Carol A. Pemberton. This listing is reprinted courtesy of UMI Research Press, Ann Arbor, Michigan. Full titles, publication data, and annotations appear in of the Catalog of Works above; code numbers refer to listings in that catalog. Initial dates of publication and co-editors (where applicable) are indicated in parentheses.

Church Music

The Hymnist (serial, 1849, William Mason) W81
Cantica Laudis (1859, Webb) W82
The Hymnist (1850) W84
The New Carmina Sacra (1850) W85
Congregational Church Music (1852-53, Novello et al.) W88
Mason's Hand-Book of Psalmody (1852) W89
The Hallelujah (1854) W90
The Sabbath Hymn and Tune Book (1859, Park, Phelps) W101
The People's Tune Book (1860) W103
The New Sabbath Hymn and Tune Book (1866, Park, Phelps) W107
Carmina Sacra Enlarged: The American Tune Book (1869) W109
Congregational Church Music (1869, Novello et al.) W110

Children's Books

The Juvenile Psalmist (1829) W6
The Juvenile Lyre (1831, Ives) W10
Sabbath School Songs (1833) W16
The Sabbath School Harp (1836) W32
The Juvenile Singing School (1837, Webb) W34
The Juvenile Songster (1837-38?) W39
Juvenile Music (1839) W43
Little Songs for Little Singers (1840) W45
The Boston School Song Book (1841) W47
The American Sabbath School Singing Book (1843) W61
The Primary School Song Book (1846, Webb) W74
The Song-Book of the School-Room (1847, Webb) W76
The Song Garden, Parts I and II (1864) W106
The Song Garden, Part III (1866) W106

Glee and Part-Song Books; Choral Works

The Boston Academy's Collection of Choruses (1836) W27
Selections for the Choir of the Boston Academy (1836) W33
The Odeon (1837, Webb) W35
The Boston Glee Book (1838) W36
The Lyrist (1838, Webb) W37
The Gentlemen's Glee Book (1841) W49
Twenty-One Madrigals, Glees, and Part Songs (1843, Webb) W65
The Vocalist (1844, Webb) W69

Individual, Sheet Music Publications

Miscellaneous

Alphabetical Listing of Works

An Excerpt from Mason's Writings

The following passages are quoted verbatim from "How Shall I Teach? or Hints to Teachers as the the Use of 'Music and Its Notation,' as Found in the *Diapason, a Collection of Church Music*, by Mr. Geo. F. Root." *Some paragraphs have been divided for readability, but the presentation follows the overall order of the original.*

[In] "Music and Its Notation," we have endeavored to present the common facts...taking it for granted that pedagogic art and science are already at the teacher's command, and that he will, therefore, be able to draw out and direct the powers of his pupils in a natural way, by such appeals to their senses, powers of reasoning, and faith, as the subject may require.

It is, perhaps, a matter of little consequence whether instruction in music commences with Rhythmics or Melodics, since the two departments must soon be combined and proceed together....We have presented the former first in order....No good teacher will allow himself to be fettered by routine, but will adapt himself to the circumstances of his class. The place where Dynamics may be introduced has not been indicated, but since the cultivation of taste should receive careful attention from the beginning, and since that cultivation is essentially dependent upon this department,...it should certainly be not long delayed....

We would not commence with book rules, nor attempt to lead from general laws to particular facts, but rather from particular facts to general laws; not from theory to practice, but from practice to theory. It will be understood...that we attempt to give a clue to that form or manner of teaching which is called Pestalozzian or inductive....Some of its leading characteristics, without any attempt at completeness or logical order,...are the following:

> 1. It looks to the inductive powers as the basis of educational work, and sees in them the germ of those faculties which are to be drawn out and made perfect.
>
> 2. It is always so directed that teaching...is made subservient to education, or to the awakening...[of] the various human powers in their relation one to another.
>
> 3. It leads the pupil to depend upon his own powers, and keeps him ever in the way of investigation.
>
> 4. It presents things before signs; leading the pupil to the practical knowledge of realities before names or symbols are given, or definitions are required.
>
> 5. It is not dependent upon books, but always prefers an oral to a book-lesson.
>
> 6. It simplifies the elements of knowledge, and would reduce every thing to its primitive component parts.
>
> 7. It always commences with something practically known, proceeding from this to the unknown.
>
> 8. Its steps are carefully graduated, and by frequent reviews are linked closely together as the work advances.
>
> 9. As an indispensable requisite in all right teaching, it makes every thing pleasant and agreeable to the pupil; and it does this legitimately, by keeping him on the track of research and discovery, thus causing his gratification to be derived from the pursuit and attainment of knowledge.
>
> 10. To whatever department of study it is applied, it seeks to put forth a right physical, intellectual and moral influence, and thus to lead to the highest human development.

As the good teacher must proceed in his work much in a conversational way, or by question and answer, we have... [given] specimens of such questions....We hope no one will suppose that questions *in these very words* are necessary, or [that] any other questions or answers are to be committed to memory and then recited. Such...can be of little value. Questions ...should not be intended to appeal to the memory merely, but mostly to awaken attention and thought, and to excite to greater activity of mental effort.

[**An Example: Introducing Rhythm**] *First Step*. (Realities) The teacher may sing before his class...the syllable LA...eight times....The tones should be distinctly and clearly given, and *staccato* should be carefully avoided. When this has been repeated once or twice..., he may ask, "How many *times* did I sing *la*?" The pupils will reply, "Eight times." After another repetition or two, the class may be required to do the same thing, or to sing *la* eight times, as the teacher did.

The class should be silent and attentive when the teacher sings, and the teacher should be silent and attentive when the class sing. Let the same example be repeated until it becomes familiar, now to the syllable *la* and then to other monosyllables, as NO, COME, GO, STAY, etc. Thus it will be perceived that the class commence not by learning rules, definitions, names or signs, but by singing; not by *notes* but by *tones*.

Second Step. Measures. (Realities). The teacher may sing as before, but dropping the monosyllables...he now sings in connection with counting thus:--ONE, TWO; ONE, TWO; ONE, TWO; ONE, TWO. After the pupils have done the same thing (teacher listening) the question may be asked,... "What have we now *added* to our first lesson?" Ans. "Counting." "How many *times* did we count two in singing the lesson?" Ans. "Four times."

Third Step. (Names and Definitions) The lesson having been repeated, the teacher may say, "In counting as we now have done, we indicate or mark a portion of time as it passes, which portion of time is called technically A MEASURE." He may then ask "What is a *portion of time* called?" Ans. "A measure." "What is a *measure*?" Ans. "A portion of time."..."What is a *shorter portion of time* than a measure called?" Ans. "A part of a measure." "How many tones have we sung *in a measure*?" Ans. "Two." "How many to *each part* of a measure?" Ans. "One." "How is a measure *indicated*?" Ans. "By counting."

[Subsequent steps:] *Fourth Step*. Accent. (Realities) *Fifth Step*. Beating Time. (Incidentals) *Sixth Step*. Beating Time. (Names and Definitions) *Seventh Step*. Notes. (Signs) *Eighth Step*. Bars. (Signs)*Ninth Step*. Resting. (Realities)*Tenth Step*. Rests. (Signs)

Let the lesson be made familiar by repetition, sometimes a little slower and sometimes a little quicker, and by questions and answers....Definitions are not...intended to include a full view of the subject, or to cover the whole ground, but only to correspond with the knowledge of the pupils, extending no further than they have been made acquainted with...to be completed as progress is made in that practical knowledge which should always precede mere verbal explanations....

[An Example: Introducing Note Reading] Chapter III. Melodics. (Review.) ...while the pupils count and beat time, [the teacher] may sing the lessons he has written [in quarter notes, not on the staff] to the syllable *la, but now to the pitch of c*. This change of pitch is important...[because] the pupils at the very start [of their study of melody]...may also commence the acquisition of the practical knowledge of absolute pitch, which is quite essential to their highest success afterwards. It is not necessary...that any thing should be said to the pupils [on this matter].... Let them now sing their...lessons in c; thus this pitch will soon become familiar, and a habit will be formed by which it will be fixed in the mind....

First Step. Tones One and Two. (Realities) While the pupils count and beat time, the teacher sings...but in the third measure, instead of the pitch c, he raises his voice to d, singing d in the third measure, and returning to c again, closing with it in the fourth measure. After a repetition, he asks, "Did the tones appear to be the *same in pitch* throughout the lesson, or was there any change?" Ans. "There was a change." "A change of *what*?" Ans. "Of pitch." "In which *measure* was the change?" "In the third measure." "Did the pitch in the third measure appear to be *higher* or *lower* than in the other?" Ans. "Higher."

After a repetition of the lesson by the teacher, the class may be required to sing it. Let it not be forgotten, that when the teacher sings the pupils should count and beat time, and *vice versa*.

Second Step. (Names). Teacher says, "Having now become acquainted with two tones of different *pitch*, we will give names to them; the name of the lower tone may be ONE, and the name of the higher tone TWO. What is the name of the *lower* tone?" Ans. "One." "What is the name of the *higher* tone?" Ans. "Two." "*What is* the lower tone?"

In answer to this question, the pupils should...sing the pitch c; whether they do so or not will probably depend... upon their previous educational habits. If they have been accustomed to discriminate between *things and signs of things*,...they will do so; but if they have not been accustomed thus..., they may not understand the question. The good teacher will not let this or any other opportunity pass of bringing out and confirming all such distinctions. He will, therefore, repeat the question, varying, perhaps, its form: "*What* is one?" "*What* is the reality?" or "*What* is the tone whose name is one?" &c. The distinction between the tone and its name must be made clear.

Such exercises as the following will help to fix in the minds of the pupils the difference of pitch between the tones One and Two. Teacher says, "Sing One." Pupils sing *la*. "Sing Two."

Pupils sing, also to *la*. Teacher says, "Name the tones which I sing." He then sings, now *One, (la)* and now *Two, (la)*, continually changing, and the pupils name the tone as soon as they hear it....

Third Step. The Staff Commenced. (Signs). The teacher says, "I will now proceed to represent or to indicate by writing, the pitch of these tones, One and Two, in accordance with common usage." He makes a line [a horizontal line is inserted] and pointing, says, "the *line* may represent the tone One, and the *space above the line* may represent the tone Two."

He now calls upon the pupils to sing as he points; pointing to the line they sing One...or to the space and they sing Two..... Little tunes, composed by the teacher from these two tones, may now be introduced, and at this point be sung by the pupils to a line or more of poetry. The pupils now sing *by note*.

[**Subsequent Steps:**] *Fourth Step*. The Succession of Tones Indicated by Notes in Connection with the Line or Space. (Signs). *Fifth Step*. One, Two, and Three. *Sixth Step*. One, Two, Three, and Four. *Seventh Step*. One, Two, Three, Four, and Five. *Eighth Step*. One, Two, Three, Four, Five, Six, Seven and Eight. *Ninth Step*. The Scale Represented in Different Positions on the Staff.

...The object of these notes to teachers has not been to give a full exposition of a method of teaching, but only briefly to touch upon certain prominent topics...; if these hints shall lead to reflection on the part of teachers, or those who desire to become teachers, or to the study of the pedagogic art, or manner of teaching, we shall be abundantly satisfied and rewarded.

Index

Page numbers refer to the pages in the Biography or other sections of this book. Numbers preceded by a *W* refer to works in the Catalog of Works; numbers preceded by a *B* refer to works in the Bibliography.

About the Author

CAROL A. PEMBERTON is an English Instructor at Norman-
dale Community College in Bloomington, Minnesota. Her published works include *Lowell Mason: His Life and Work* along
with articles in such publications as *The Bulletin of Historical
Research in Music Education*, *Music Educators Journal* and the
Journal of Research in Music Education.